Theodoret of Cyrrhus

Theodoret of Cyrrhus

The Bishop and the Holy Man

THERESA URBAINCZYK

Ann Arbor

THE UNIVERSITY OF MICHIGAN PRESS

2005   2004   2003   2002   4   3   2   1

Library of Congress Cataloging-in-Publication Data

Urbainczyk, Theresa, 1960–
    Theodoret of Cyrrhus : the bishop and the holy man /
Theresa Urbainczyk.
        p.   cm.
    Includes bibliographical references and index.
    ISBN 0-472-11266-X (alk. paper)
    1. Theodoret, Bishop of Cyrrhus.   I. Title.
BR1720.T36 U73   2002
270.2′092 — dc21
    [B]   2002020247

For Jeanne Glenz and Mary Holland

Acknowledgments

I would like to thank University College Dublin, and its Classics Department, especially Andrew Smith, for allowing me to take two periods of sabbatical leave, in Germany and the United States, without which this book would still be merely a file of notes. In Munich Franz Tinnefeld gave very useful advice on an early draft. In New York Alan Camaron told me all I needed to know to survive in Manhattan, lent me a bike, and gave scholarly comments on my work. I cannot imagine what would have happened to me without his hospitality and that of the Classics Department of Columbia University. I am also indebted to Richard Price, not only for his invaluable translation of the *Religious History* but for his wise and learned remarks on what I wrote. Kieran Allen, Kevin Cathcart, Jan Willem Drijvers, Andrew Erskine, and Marina Greatrex also waded their way patiently through versions of this work and offered constructive criticism when it was much needed. I am also indebted to two anonymous readers for the University of Michigan Press for their advice. All errors are of my own creation.

Vic Connerty, Jeanne Glenz, Mary Holland, Gwen Ellison, Barbara Forbes, Scott Fraser, Catherine Johnston, and Catherine O'Dea all kept me going in the right direction. No one could wish for a more enthusiastic and encouraging editor than Collin Ganio and I am extremely grateful to him for enthusing me when I was getting a little tired of Theodoret.

It is thanks to my family that I have always understood why some people might wish to flee human society forever. It is only relatively recently, however, that I have gained some grasp of why anyone might have the urge to write hagiography, and I dedicate this book to two modern equivalents of holy women.

Contents

PART I

Setting the Scene

Introduction

Theodoret, the bishop of Cyrrhus, is a major figure of the fifth century. His *Religious History* is a key text for understanding not only his life but the issues involved with the church in this period. When the church was realizing its full political potential, Theodoret was both an actor and an observer, helping to shape events with his observations. The *Religious History* is a remarkable document, with a wealth of personal information about its author. Most of the information we have about Theodoret's life comes from this work, with extra details gleaned from his letters.[1] He often provokes strong opinions, being referred to as "one of the noblest figures in the intellectual struggles of the Eastern church," "a highly attractive individual," or more critically "however unpleasant Theodoretus may be at times, his is a very genuine voice."[2]

Almost ten years ago I decided to study the *Ecclesiastical History* of Theodoret. This book is a result of that decision, but it is not what I originally intended. In an attempt to place the *Ecclesiastical History* in its historical context, I began to learn more about Theodoret's life, a process that quickly led me to the *Religious History,* the text that forms the focus of what follows. The *Religious History* contains information about Syria and Theodoret as well as Syrian holy men and women, but it also raises questions to which I could find no immediate answers.

1. On Theodoret's life, see Canivet 1977, 37–63. Information can also be found in Bardenhewer 1924, 219–23; Azéma 1955, 13–25; Canivet 1958; Festugière 1959, 246–47, n. 1; Quasten 1960, 536–54; Canivet and Leroy-Molinghen 1977, 9–18; Altaner 1978, 339–41; and Young 1983, 266–71. For a good example of how accepted Theodoret's account of himself is, see Gallico 1995, 24–32.

2. Grillmeier 1975, 488; Young 1983, 266; Momigliano 1990, 143–44.

On the surface it is easy to say what *Religious History* is about; it is a series of lives of Syrian holy men told by Theodoret, who had known them either when he was young in Antioch or when he was bishop of Cyrrhus and to some extent was responsible for them as members of his flock. What I learned from the work was that Theodoret was a very pious child of an equally pious mother, a woman who saw the error of her former glamorous ways and became almost too ascetic for her own good. Theodoret grew up to become a caring and concerned bishop who had the respect of the devout individuals about whom he was writing and who often took better care of them than they took of themselves. He tended his sheep, even those who had wandered off into the desert, so to speak.[3]

On the other hand, I also got the impression from his work that the holy men themselves were extreme, perhaps foolishly so, and rather self-obsessed, looking only to their own salvation by punishing themselves in elaborate and imaginative ways. They were also sometimes rather rude if not downright objectionable. In other words, Theodoret emerged from this hagiography more virtuous than his heroes, which struck me as a little odd. It could be that he was profoundly vain, a vice not unknown in men of the cloth, or it could be that he was not a very good hagiographer. I had my doubts about both explanations.

We know much more about Theodoret than his contemporaries, Socrates and Sozomen, who also wrote church histories. This is because we have other, in fact many other, extant works by him and also because he was an active participant in the church politics of the day. The first half of the fifth century saw theological disputes polarized around the sees of Antioch and Alexandria. Being a bishop, unlike Socrates or Sozomen, he took part in these disputes and the church councils in which differences were aired. For his pains, he was forbidden to travel outside his see. This was clearly not sufficient for his enemies, so he was then deposed but reinstated and finally, a hundred years after his death, had some of his works condemned. The rough division was between Antioch in Syria and Alexandria in Egypt.

---

3. Most secondary material accepts Theodoret's words unquestioningly. The latest example of this approach is Escolan 1999; another is Trombley 1995, 143–73 (e.g., "There is little doubt that Theodoret's observations are sound," he remarks on p. 150). Leppin (1996a, 217) reads the text more carefully, however, observing that Theodoret portrays his own relationship with these monks as unproblematic.

Egypt was famous for its monks. Theodoret was on the Antiochene side. Therefore, one reason not to dismiss Theodoret summarily as conceited or clumsy is that there were similar works circulating at the time celebrating the lives of Egyptian monks. It is a reasonable supposition that the *Religious History* might be a riposte to those other glorifications, an assertion that Syria, as well as Egypt, had produced models of holiness.

This did not solve the issue of Theodoret's personal appearances in the *Religious History,* however. For this it seemed to me necessary to examine his career to see what he might have been aiming to achieve with this work. Momigliano has observed that one has to distinguish what the biographer tells about his subject and what he wants to say for himself.[4] It seemed very clear that there were things Theodoret wished to say about himself, and it did not seem satisfactory to label this as narcissism. While on the one hand it is true that Theodoret was drawing the reader closer to his topic by asserting his own intimacy with his subjects, the nature of that intimacy seemed rather unexpected.[5] It was by no means inevitable that Theodoret would portray his subjects as being in a position so deferential to himself. Given his active role in the controversies of the day, the probability that this work was part of the debate seemed high.[6]

There were other issues that I felt needed to be investigated before one could properly understand the text. Theodoret draws attention to the fact that some of the individuals he is describing spoke only Syriac. He also lets us know that he understands this language, although the text of the *Religious History* is in Greek, the Greek of a highly educated man. While it is not surprising that the Roman Empire contained many other languages besides Latin and Greek, that fact is often forgotten and yet in this text we have an author drawing attention to it. Because this is unusual — that is, it is relatively rare that we learn directly about the native languages of the empire — it seemed fruitful to look at Theodoret's intention in raising the topic.

Women play a considerable part in the work, not least Theodoret's own mother. Indeed, the final three lives discussed are those of female ascetics. In classical literature women are either invisible

---

4. Momigliano 1987, 165.

5. Ibid., 177.

6. Martin (1993) remarks about Athanasius's *Apologies* that despite first appearances the work reveals very little personal information about the author himself.

or used as foils for men. However, Theodoret's women are not beautiful temptresses or treacherous murderers but appear to be realistic late antique women in Syria. Appearances can be deceptive, however, and it was necessary to look carefully at how Theodoret represents women and what he describes them as doing and to observe how they differ from their male counterparts.

Members of the clergy also have a role to play in the *Religious History,* and from even a cursory reading of it there emerges a very definite attitude of respectful regard on the part of these otherwise rather rebellious ascetics towards clergymen. Indeed, this respect seemed to be emphasized, so I have been concerned to examine every instance of the interaction between the ascetics and representatives of the established church.

Connected to this is the attitude Theodoret reveals toward the very practice of asceticism, which leads us to the earlier point that one sometimes receives an almost disapproving picture of these figures. At certain points in the work Theodoret seems to express an ambiguous attitude toward the activities of those whom he purports to praise. This in itself seemed to reveal a tension in the work that can also be found in other hagiographic texts.

Asceticism is the subject of much scholarly debate.[7] One might view the asceticism of the desert fathers as the complete negation of the ideal life of the classical world, as it is presented, for instance, by Aristotle, since these people left the polis, left society, seeking solitude in order to gain entrance to a higher level of being. Asceticism itself, however, was not simply a Christian phenomenon.[8] Many philosophical groups had turned from luxury to a life of discipline.[9] People endured the most remarkable hardships because they believed they were acquiring something infinitely more valuable than

---

7. See, for instance, Wimbush and Valantasis 1995. See also Clark 2000 on pagan asceticism.

8. See Elliott 1987, 90–91, 173, on asceticism as a rejection of the political life. See Nock 1933; Chadwick 1985, 1; and Wimbush 1986 on early manifestations of the ascetic life. As Bagnall remarks rather dryly, "The renunciation of sexual activity is certainly a subject unlikely to find anyone without an opinion" (1993, 294). See Brown 1998b on pagan and Christian asceticism. Francis (1995) provides a thorough and thought-provoking study of pagan asceticism; see especially his final chapter, "Ascetics and Holy Men."

9. This was charted by Nock (1933). See also Wimbush 1985, 18, discussing Brown 1980. Brown had argued for a radical distinction between the pagan philosopher and the Christian ascetic since the philosopher worked within society whereas the Christian holy man worked from without.

worldly comfort and success.[10] It is also a rejection of that worldly comfort and success.[11]

Holy men, almost paradoxically, could be rather dangerous figures for the established church. Or perhaps one might say that individuals before they were sanctified by the church could be rather dangerous. Writing about them was perhaps a way of diffusing the threat or containing it. Independents who went off by themselves and attracted their own followings could be quite powerful local figures. They were operating on the principles that the church espoused and yet, since Constantine, could be seen as betraying. Consequently, those within the church were eager to either eliminate their rivals or, far more effectively, claim them for themselves and draw them into the ecclesiastical fold. This need not necessarily lead to condemnation of their activities; the message in the *Religious History,* I would argue, is that extreme forms of asceticism were not to be encouraged. There should be moderation even in one's religious zeal. Symeon Stylites, the man who lived atop a column for years, is the most famous of all Theodoret's heroes, yet the critical tone is most noticeable in this life.

Christians made very good use of biography to get their message across. They used it because of its simplicity — the structure is comprehensible to everyone, following a person's life from cradle to grave. Pagans, perhaps recognizing its force, also used it to glorify their philosophers, and we get a spate of biographies of late antique pagan holy men as well as Christian ones. Momigliano has pointed out that the difference between the two is the presence of the bishop in the lives of the Christian versions.[12] Although he was not talking about Theodoret at the time, he could not have made a more apposite comment about the *Religious History.* The work is usually consulted because in it Theodoret gives us information about himself that he

10. Elm 1994, 13.

11. Markus (1990, 165) describes the attractions of the desert: "Cassian claimed to be following the monastic leaders of Egypt. But he had a far sharper awareness that the ascetic life was a vivid comment on the society from which the monk seceded. The immense silence of the Desert, the *eremi vastitas* constantly spoken of by the monastic writers, was the potent symbol of a break with the organized societies of Roman city-life. To enter the Desert was to assert one's freedom to extricate oneself from the suffocating bonds of that society, from the claims of property relationships, of power and domination, of marriage and family and to recreate a life of primal freedom, whether in solitude or in an alternative and freely chosen social grouping."

12. Momigliano 1987, 177.

gives us nowhere else. Until now, this has been interpreted as giving the work authenticity: Theodoret is letting the reader know that he knows what he is talking about. However, I would argue that there were other ways he could have done this, methods used by the authors of the *History of the Monks of Egypt* and the *Lausiac History*. The *Religious History* is different, and I hope this will become clear by the end of this work.

The *Religious History* has been studied extensively by Pierre Canivet, who edited and translated the text with Alice Leroy-Molinghen for *Sources Chrétiennes* and went on to write *Le Mona-chisme Syrien selon Théodoret de Cyr* as well as a series of articles about the text. My own examination is of a different nature, but the debt I owe to Canivet's writings will be very clear in the following pages.

Theodoret has left us with this very positive image of himself.[13] He did this very skillfully, and it has been my aim to indicate just how carefully he composed this work. Part I gives the historical and literary background, with an overall description of the *Religious History* and Theodoret's stated aims for his composition (chapters 1–4). Part II is an examination of how Theodoret presents his heroes, their social status, and their activities. They came from a range of backgrounds; one was a man who had given up a post in the imperial service, while another was an uneducated shepherd who knew no Greek. Some performed miracles; others did virtually nothing. Some helped women; others would not allow members of the opposite sex anywhere near them. I discuss Symeon Stylites separately, as he is the most famous holy man of them all and Theodoret gives him a much longer account than any of the others bar one (chapters 5–9).

Part III proceeds to scrutinize the ways in which Theodoret portrayed the relationship between these ascetics and the church, as

---

13. The scholar most recently charmed by Theodoret is Krueger, who suggests we should view the work as an act of piety in itself (1997a). By representing himself so frequently throughout the work, Theodoret is showing himself to be a devotee of these individuals: "A rhetoric of piety is embedded in the *Religious History*'s structure" (711). At the end of each life Theodoret asks for the blessing of the holy man (for himself) and, says Krueger, by using very similar words each time Theodoret shows that he sees them as canonical gestures, like reciting the doxology at the end of psalms or making a sign of the cross. Krueger sees Theodoret writing his *Religious History* as an act of piety similar to going on a pilgrimage, giving food to saints, or asking them for healing, blessing, or intercession (712). This is exactly what Theodoret would have us think. He virtually spells this out all the way through the text.

represented by priests, bishops, and himself. Clergymen appear regularly in the pages of the *Religious History,* as does Theodoret. I argue that this is not incidental but central to gaining an understanding what he was trying to convey in his text. Theodoret wanted to show that he was an extraordinary bishop with an army of remarkable monks behind him, the equal of any Egyptian. To the upper classes of the big cities these were wild men from the Syrian mountains. To Theodoret they were devoted and loyal. To anyone in authority whom they considered unjust they were utterly fearless and bellicose. With God manifestly on their side they were potent allies of their embattled bishop.

Chapter 1

Theodoret's Life and Times

Theodoret was deposed by a church council, reinstated by another, and, many years after his death, had his writings condemned by a third. From such a career one can safely assume that he had many enemies and held theological views unpalatable to those in power in the church. People make enemies because of their theological views. Conversely, to take a rather cynical view, it could be argued that one can be assigned unpalatable theological views by one's enemies as part of a hostile process. In addition, both may be true. Without entering into this discussion, there is no doubt that the first half of the fifth century saw vigorous disagreements between the Antiochene and Alexandrian churches. Theodoret was on the Antiochene side and had enemies in the Egyptian camp.

We do not know when he was born. One certain date is that of his consecration as bishop in 423, to which he refers specifically in various letters.[1] It is usually asserted that he was born in 393 although there is no precise evidence for this.[2] In 449 he speaks of his old age in a letter to Leo (*Epistle* 113) and if born in 393 he would have been fifty-six at the time. In letter 116, which was written in the same year, he refers to his old age and gray hair; again he is writing to ask for support against his enemies. Given that he is protesting his ill treatment and hoping that Leo will support him, it is quite probable that he would describe himself in this way at that time. It seems reason-

---

1. In *Epistle* 80 and 81, written in 448 when he was confined to his see, he says that he has been bishop for twenty-five years. In *Epistle* 113 and 116, written in 449, he says that he has been bishop for twenty-six years.

2. See, for example, Price 1985, ix; and Blomfield Jackson [1892], 1994, 1, following Tillemont. There is a more considered discussion in Canivet 1977, 39, esp. n. 13.

able to accept somewhere around 393 as his date of birth, and he would therefore have been thirty years old in 423 when he was appointed bishop of Cyrrhus.

The Empire

His life might be characterized as beginning with a division of the empire and ending with a division of the church. In 395 Theodosius I died, leaving his two young sons, Arcadius and Honorius, as rulers of the empire, with Arcadius given the eastern part and Honorius the western.[3] From that time on, the empire was effectively divided into two administrative areas, which today are usually studied separately. The last Roman emperor in the west was deposed in 476 whereas the east survived as the Byzantine Empire for another thousand years.

East and west had been administered separately since Diocletian (284–305), but under some emperors there had been a reunification. After the death of Theodosius I, the separation was final, although Justinian attempted to reverse it in the sixth century. Constantinople, since the time of Constantine, had a new importance as well as a new name. It possessed all the necessary political structures to take over from Rome, including its own senate and consul.

Theodoret lived in the safer half of the empire and as far as we know never traveled west. When he was in his late teens Alaric and his soldiers sacked Rome, the Eternal City;[4] by the time he was in his late thirties the Vandals had invaded and conquered Africa, the grain supplier of the empire. Britain and northern Gaul were also lost to the Romans, and there were barbarians living in communities independent of the Romans but within their borders.

In contrast, the east was relatively calm, the main storms being

---

3. Both have received very harsh judgments from modern scholars (see, e.g., Jones 1964, 173: "Arcadius and Honorius were personally decent, respectable men, but weak and sluggish"). Two years later, he was even harsher (Jones 1966, 74: "Both [Arcadius and Honorius] proved feeble and lazy characters when they grew up") Or see Blockley 1998, 136, on Honorius: "The kindest thing that can be said about this most ineffective incumbent upon the imperial throne is that his long periods of inertia caused less damage than his bouts of relative activity just before and after the destruction of Stilicho."

4. See Woods 2000, 123–32, for a novel interpretation of one of the aspects of this event.

ecclesiastical. When Theodosius I died, he left a series of laws reinforcing the position of Nicene Christianity and severely limiting the lives of anyone with different beliefs.[5] Such measures of course did not end theological discussions and disputes, which in turn gave rise to councils, depositions, and reinstatements. Theodoret would have been in his midteens when the seven-year-old Theodosius II, the grandson of his namesake, ascended the throne on the death of his father, Arcadius, in 408. Theodosius II's reign was surprisingly long and peaceful and only ended in 450 because he fell off his horse.[6] Being so young when he came to the throne he, like his father and uncle before him, relied heavily on advisers, one of them being his older sister Pulcheria, by whom even he was outstripped in piety and by whom he was eventually succeeded.[7] It was during Theodosius II's reign that two important church councils took place, important in the history of the church but also in the life of Theodoret; both were held in Ephesus, the first in 431 and the second in 449 (often referred to as the Latrocinium or Robber Council), by which Theodoret was deposed. Virtually the last piece of information we have about him is that he was reinstated two years later at the Council of Chalcedon in 451, which in fact marked the beginning of a more pronounced split within the church than had previously been the case.[8]

In 398, while Theodoret was still a child visiting holy men with his mother, one of the local preachers, John Chrysostom, left Antioch, having been appointed bishop of the eastern capital, Constantinople. Within six years John had been deposed, reinstated, and exiled, and three years later was dead, brought down by the deadly combination of Pulcheria's grandmother and the machinations of a rival bishop,

---

5. "Theodosius was a fanatical persecutor of heretics" (Jones 1966, 70).

6. Blomfield Jackson, in his introduction to the *Nicene and Post-Nicene Fathers,* comments "Now, not for the last time in history, an important part was played by a horse" ([1892] 1994, 9).

7. It is interesting to see the shift in the way this woman has been described. In 1964 Jones said "By the time that Theodosius II died, leaving no male heir, a strong dynastic sentiment had grown up, and his successor, Marcian, thought it wise to strengthen his position by marrying Pulcheria" (1964, 174), whereas Cameron (1993b, 23) has "Theodosius II was replaced by Marcian, an elderly soldier whom Pulcheria chose for her husband." De Halleux's empress is also much more formidable than Jones's (1993, 7): "Succédant à son frère, Pulchérie épouse le général Marcien, fait exécuter Chrysaphe, interner Eutychès et repatrier le corps de Flavien, qui avait succombé sur le chemin de l'exil." See Holum (1982, 209), who describes Pulcheria's consort as "her illicit lover, the young and handsome Marcian."

8. Halleux 1993, 3.

Theophilus of Alexandria, if the church historians are to be believed. The nephew of Theophilus, Cyril, succeeded his uncle in the Egyptian see. If one combines the length of the occupancy by uncle and nephew, they controlled the key position in the Egyptian church for half a century. Cyril was to be responsible for the downfall of Theodoret, which took place just before Theodosius II suffered his own.

There is another parallel. In 425 another Antiochene, Nestorius, was elevated to the see of Constantinople. Within six years he had been deposed and forced to retire to a monastery. Both he and John suffered the enmity of the bishop of Alexandria, Theophilus in the case of John and Cyril for Nestorius. The dispute that brought down Nestorius was one in which Theodoret was involved and is discussed later in this chapter. Compared to the barbarian invasions in the west, these upsets were perhaps less deadly but the aftereffects were long lasting. The role of the bishop had developed enormously in the fourth century, and the incumbents of prominent sees held considerable power. It was therefore a matter of great consequence who held certain sees. The Alexandrians objected when Syrians were appointed to the see of Constantinople and thus went to considerable trouble to oust John and Nestorius.

The same period also witnessed a phenomenal increase in the number of people joining monasteries, and these communities quickly came to wield no small influence themselves.[9] It can be confusing to talk about *monasticism* in the context of Theodoret's *Religious History* and during this early period, since the later manifestations of this phenomenon tend to color our interpretations of this word. For many today the word *monasteries* evokes an image of highly organized and disciplined bodies at the service of the church hierarchy. In late antiquity, such developments were still in the future and the terms *monk, ascetic,* and *holy man* are here used interchangeably. The word *monk* comes from the Greek *monachos,* which means "solitary," so it is one of those strange quirks of language that later the word came to be used to describe someone who lives with others in a community, whereas *holy man* is usually employed for those who lived by themselves. The individuals Theodoret described usually lived at least part of their lives in solitude as well as in groups, as will be discussed later.

The adoption of asceticism, either individually or in the society of

---

9. See Dunn 2000 for a convenient overview of the growth of monasticism.

like-minded others, was not exclusively Christian, as has often been observed.[10] Strands of philosophy had often advocated some form of askesis, and there were ascetic communities in the Jewish tradition. However, what was peculiarly Christian was the enormous numbers involved, beginning in the fourth century. Communities of several thousand were reported as commonplace in Egypt. Although there is always the tendency to wish to avoid simplistic explanations, it hardly seems a coincidence that the escalation in the numbers of people leaving their homes to lead lives more in keeping with the Gospels, or at least in the ways they interpreted them, took place at the same time that Christianity was receiving more acceptance from the imperial authorities and playing an increasingly political role in society at large.[11] Ascetic practices in Syria are often characterized as especially harsh, and certainly stylitism, that is, living on a column, which by any definition would seem to be particularly tough, seems to have originated there. The first stylite we know of, Symeon, who is the subject of the twenty-sixth life of the *Religious History,* was virtually an exact contemporary of Theodoret.

Theodoret in Antioch

Theodoret came from Antioch, a place of major importance and influence in the late Roman world. It was one of the largest cities of the empire, being a commercial center, the capital of Roman Syria, and an imperial base during the fourth century.[12] It had a large Jewish community and also held an extremely significant place in the

10. See, for instance, Brown 1998.

11. Dunn (2000, 1) appears to distance herself from such interpretations, although she does not proffer an alternative one. Brown takes a characteristically individualist approach: "At this time the principal division within the Christian community was less between a clearly defined 'ascetic movement' and all other Christians, than between those who had decided to undergo the drastic rite of baptism" (1998b, 618). In this piece he paints a rather improbable picture of late antique society, both Christian and pagan, as predominantly pious and ascetic.

12. For a clear, precise, and concise overview of Antioch in antiquity, see Wallace-Hadrill 1982, 1–12. Much has been written on this celebrated city. See, for instance, Festugière 1959; Downey 1961; and Liebeschuetz 1972. See also Sartre 1991, 328–32, on the villages of northern Syria and 339–49 on Antioch. See Jones 1971, 241–44, 252, 263, 268, 293, on Theodoret's area. The Syrian economy seems to have been a flourishing one from the third to the sixth centuries (Garnsey 1996, 121–42).

history of the church, for it was in Antioch that Greeks converted en masse and became known as Christians (Acts 11.26). It was one of the main sees, the others being Alexandria, Constantinople, Jerusalem, and Rome.[13] It was a Greek foundation, founded by Seleucus I, one of Alexander's generals, and its inhabitants, or at least the upper classes of them, spoke Greek.

In the eastern half of the empire, Greek was the language of administration and literature, just as Latin was in the west. On one level, the empire had always been divided (linguistically) since, although the official language of the government, army, and law was Latin, the upper classes continued to speak Greek in the east. It is easy to forget the myriad of other tongues that were spoken throughout the empire simply because most of them were not written down.[14] How far knowledge of Greek spread outside the city walls of Antioch is impossible to know, but thanks to Christian writers giving us a glimpse of a world beyond the one that is so familiar from pagan sources we know that the mass of the population of Syria, both outside and inside the towns of the area, continued to speak their native language, Syriac.[15] Jerome says of Syria that one had to learn a barbarous language or stay silent (*Epistle* 7.1–2). John Chrysostom speaks of those from the countryside coming into Antioch on feast days as "a people foreign to us in language, but in harmony with us in faith" (*Homily on the Statues* 19.2).[16]

The details included by Theodoret about his environs fit perfectly Sebastian Brock's picture of a linguistic and cultural overlap with no clear boundaries. Brock reasonably suggests a range of bilingualism from monoglot Greek speakers to bilinguals who only wrote Greek

13. In this period there was no agreed order of the main sees. See Gahbauer 1993, 34–35, 75–78, on the church historians Socrates, Sozomen, and Theodoret. As Gahbauer (75) points out, Theodoret gives two different orders in his church history (*Ecclesiastical History* 1.3, 5.40), although in both cases the first two bishoprics mentioned are Rome followed by Antioch.

14. For an overview of the languages of the area, see Elton's forthcoming book on Cilicia, appendix 5. See also Drijvers 1998.

15. See Brock 1994; and Downey 1961, 534. Jones describes the situation neatly: "Culturally the country-side remained utterly unaffected by the Hellenism of the cities; the peasants continued to speak Syriac down to the Arab conquest" (1971, 294). Millar is far more cautious (see, e.g., 1998a, 74; 1993, 229–30; and 1971, 7), although see also Millar 1998b. I use the conventional term *Syriac* (which Theodoret also uses) to refer to the language native to Antioch and Cyrrhus, despite Millar's reservations (1971, 6). He prefers the word *Aramaic* except when referring to the dialect spoken around Edessa.

16. See Jones 1964, 991–96; and 1971, 241–94, on the area.

to non-Greek speakers. He also remarks that the Syriac language seems to have been rather despised as "barbaric" east of the Euphrates, whereas it was a respected literary language west of the river.[17]

If some inhabitants of Antioch only spoke Syriac, or spoke it predominantly, it is likely that the Greek-speaking ones would have picked up some of the language.[18] Theodoret makes it quite clear in the *Religious History* that he and his family knew Syriac; his mother took him to see holy men who spoke only Syriac, implying that she at least could converse with them in their own tongue. This does not necessarily mean it was her or his first language, which seems unlikely given the nature of Theodoret's literary Greek and his social status, which is decidedly not that of a peasant.[19] That great arbiter of linguistic skill, Photius, praised the purity of Theodoret's Attic Greek (*Bibliotheca* 31, 203), and all of his extant works are in this language.

There is nothing in the *Religious History* to help on this issue, but in the *Cure for Hellenic Maladies* Theodoret refers to his own language in a rather enigmatic way. In book 5 he makes what must have been a startling argument for some of his readers, saying that just being Greek does not mean one is virtuous. One can be virtuous without speaking Greek, and he goes on to say that the prophets and apostles had true wisdom without any knowledge of this language. He points out that arts, sciences, and warfare are all to be found among the barbarians (5.71). After acknowledging that the Romans had poets, historians, and orators, he notes that "Those who know both Latin and Greek say that the Romans are wiser in thought and more concise in expression than the Greeks."[20] He goes on:

Καὶ ταῦτα λέγω οὐ τὴν Ἑλλάδα σμικρύνων φωνήν ἧς ἀμηγεπη μετέλαχον οὐδὲ ἐναντία γε αὐτῇ ἐκτίνων τροφεῖα. [I say this not

17. Brock 1998, 714–16.

18. Liebeschuetz (1972, 62) comments reasonably that Antioch must have had a Syriac-speaking population, although we do not hear about it.

19. See Urbainczyk 2000 for a discussion of Theodoret's comments on Syriac in the *Religious History.* One possibility is that Syriac was the language of the female part of the household, the assumption being that servants would be less likely to speak Greek and women had more contact with them.

20. Ῥωμαῖοι δὲ καὶ ποιητὰς ἔσχον καὶ συγγραφέας καὶ ῥήτορας καὶ φασιν οἱ ταύτην γε κἀκείνην ἠσκημένοι τὴν γλῶτταν καὶ πυκνότερα τῶν Ἑλληνικῶν τὰ τούτων ἐνθυμήματα εἶναι καὶ ξυντομωτέρας τὰς γνώμας.

to belittle the Greek language, which is my own to some extent, nor to pay the wages of my nurse with ingratitude.] (5.74–75)

This has usually been taken to mean that Greek was not his first language.[21] However, the word ἀμηγέπη, which I have translated as "to some extent," although it can also mean "somehow or other," makes this statement a little puzzling. He would appear to be saying that Greek is not his first language, but one could also take this sentence as rather ironic given that he is writing it in Greek. He wrote this work in a very self-conscious way and commented in the preface that since he was discussing Plato and other philosophers he should try to emulate their style a little (Preface 3).

However, what I think Theodoret is doing is making a play on words on Ἕλλην, which can be translated as "pagan" but can also simply mean Greek or Hellenic.[22] The whole work is called Ἑλ-ληνικῶν θεραπευτικὴ παθημάτων, that is, *Cure for Hellenic Maladies,* but it is directed against the pagans. The word for Greek and pagan (Ἕλλην) was the same and thus the wordplay is possible in Greek but does not work in English. This is why he appears to be casting doubt on whether Greek was his language or not. He is saying that on some level his is the language of the pagans because he has had a classical education. He is acknowledging his debt to the classical writers and admitting that he does not wish to discard it all. The *Cure for Hellenic Maladies* is actually an affectionate look at the philosophers. It is a "cure" for people who are sick; he is trying to help them, to show them the error of their ways, not attack them. He gives an alternative title for the work *The Truth of the Gospel Proved from Greek Philosophy;* there is here a very definite acknowledgment of the value of previous learning.[23] Pagans are clearly much less of a threat by this period than heretics are, so Theodoret could afford to take a relaxed attitude and accept the fact that that some of them had made some good points.[24]

21. See Bardenhewer 1924, 221; Bardy 1948, 18–31, esp. 19; Canivet 1977, 38–39; and recently Brock 1998, 714.

22. Urbainczyk 1997a, 89–92; Bowersock 1990, 7–13.

23. Εὐαγγελικῆς ἀληθείας ἐξ Ἑλληνικῆς ἐπιγνωσις. The work is extremely interesting, and in the passage in which this sentence occurs he is making the point that barbarians can be as intelligent as Greeks (5.71–75).

24. Cf. Socrates (*Ecclesiastical History* 3.16.10–11), who made a similar argument discussed by me (1997a, 90–91).

The passage quoted earlier does not therefore prove that Greek is his second language. We can only state for certain that he understood Syriac and was very proficient in Greek. He does, however, seem to be saying that he does not know Latin since he writes "Those who know both Latin and Greek say that . . ." (5.74).[25] He would appear to be excluding himself from this group.

His parents were Christians and were married when Theodoret's mother was thirteen.[26] Theodoret was born when she was twenty-nine. We can infer the social standing of the family from his evident education and the social connections revealed in his correspondence. In a letter to the bishop of Rome (*Ep.* 113), he says that the whole of the east knows that he gave up his inheritance when he entered a monastery. While allowing for exaggeration, there must have been some property involved for him to say this. This impression is borne out by comments in the *Religious History,* wherein his family is portrayed as possessing servants. He mentions that his mother had taken a cook from their household to visit Peter the Galatian, the subject of the ninth life of the *Religious History* (9.9), and in the following chapter he describes his own nurse as being the grandmother of a rustic, who may well only have spoken Syriac, and taking him to see Peter (9.10). This nurse sent for Peter when Theodoret's mother was ill (9.14). In the same life he described his mother on her first visit to Peter as having been adorned with gold jewelry and silk clothing (9.6).

Another indication of his background is his evident education. His works are imbued with classical thoughts and expressions, are written in a literary style, and are clearly the products of a traditional education.[27] There are innumerable instances throughout the text of

---

25. See note 20 in this chapter.

26. Theodoret is explicit on these dates. He tells us that seven years before he was born she was twenty-two (*Religious History* 9.8) and that his parents had been married thirteen years before the father went to see Macedonius. It was four years after this that Theodoret was born (13.16). See also Canivet 1977, 37–38.

27. See Spadavecchia 1985 on the classical style of Theodoret. Bardenhewer (1924, 221–22) lists the authors Theodoret seems to have read: Homer, Plato, Isocrates, Demosthenes, Herodotus, Thucydides, Hesiod, Aristotle, Apollodorus, and Plotinus. See also Young 1983, 267; and 1997, 171. I would argue that, for instance, the following sentence is very carefully composed: ὅτι ἄνθρωπος εἴη καὶ τὴν αὐτὴν ἔχοι φύσιν τοῖς ὑβρικόσι καὶ τῇ φύσει μετρεῖν τὴν ὀργὴν δέον, ἀμέτρῳ κέχρηται τῷ θυμῷ καὶ τῶν εἰκόνων ἕνεκα τῶν οἰκείων τὰς θείας εἰκόνας σφαγῇ παραδίδωσι (That he was a man

his careful composition of sentences and the choice of a rather obscure vocabulary.[28] His learning is perhaps seen most clearly in the *Cure for Hellenic Maladies,* where he quotes extensively from classical sources in order to refute their ideas.[29] He says that he wishes to discuss the philosophers in their own style (*Preface* 3) and shows an acute consciousness of what good literary form is. He indulges in old Attic forms such as ττ instead of σσ, ξ for σ, and correctly uses ἄν and the optative and ὦ in the vocative.[30] One can see why Photius liked him.

Theodoret never mentions his formal education but reserves his recollections for his religious formation since it was his standing as a churchman that he was emphasizing.[31] So we learn from the *Religious History* that his mother and the holy men in his locality were his teachers in the matter of religion. In a letter (*Ep.* 81) he tells the consul Nomus that even before his conception his parents promised him to God and from his birth they carried out their promise and educated him accordingly. Before he was made bishop, he lived in a monastery. He raises this point to protest his not being allowed to travel and goes on to list his virtues, relating that he never took money from anyone, constructed buildings for Cyrrhus, got rid of heretics, and even shed his own blood for the church when he was stoned by heretics and nearly died. This letter has its own agenda when it discusses his education since he is trying to demonstrate how

---

with the same nature as those who had acted outrageously, that while anger ought to be proportionate to one's nature, he had given rein to anger that was out of proportion: because of his own images he was consigning to execution the images of God" [*Religious History* 13.7]).

28. I would argue he is also carefully juxtaposing πεπαιδευμένη and ἀπαιδία at *Religious History* 13.16, lines 5 and 6, perhaps simply as a pun. For other examples, see 15.5, μηνύσας τις τοῦ ἁγίου τοὺς ὅρκους τὴν ἔριν διέλυσεν (someone resolved the dispute by revealing the oaths of the saint). But the conjunction of the last two nouns cannot be accidental. Orkos was the son of Eris in mythology. Similarly, we meet the very classical metaphor of racing at 18.4 and 21.35. For other instances of wordplay and classical echoes, see 21.1 (πόνων μελέτη, which Thucydides uses of the Spartans), 21.33 (playing on the just judge), 22.5 (the medicine of faith), and 24.1 (wherein he changes a cliché about old age around).

29. See Canivet 1958, 49–58, on the sources he may have used. See also Mansfield and Runia 1997, 272–90. I am grateful to Han Baltussen for this reference. Mansfield and Runia are rather dismissive of Theodoret's erudition which they describe as secondhand.

30. His style is discussed at length by Canivet (1958, 60–67).

31. Rubenson 2000 examines the changing attitude among Christian biographers toward the issue of classical learning.

unjust his treatment has been. No one could have had a more pious upbringing nor proved his virtue so materially.

It would be naive to take details about his personal life in the *Religious History* as incidental asides. As will be discussed in chapter 11, the *Religious History* is a record of his family's friendship with the ascetics of the area. His birth occurred because his parents invoked the help of one. They were childless and asked for divine help through the prayers of Macedonius (*Religious History* 13).[32] His mother often took her small son to visit holy men and receive their blessings. Theodoret describes how he searched out one man in particular, Zeno, in order to discuss philosophy with him. As he was leaving Theodoret asked for his blessing. Zeno replied that Theodoret should pray for him since he himself was merely a civilian whereas Theodoret was a soldier, being a reader in the church. This may sound unremarkable, but Theodoret also tells us that he was very young at the time—he indicates his age by describing himself as having only recently experienced a slight growth of down on his chin (12.4).[33] It should also be noted that Theodoret is putting into Zeno's mouth the acknowledgment that even the lowest members of the church hierarchy have more claim to respect than a mere amateur. The clerics are the professionals.

Theodoret portrays his relationship with the holy men as having been very close all his life. This is an important function of the *Religious History*, to show that Theodoret from his infancy had the best possible religious instruction from none other than well-respected holy men. He, a man of the church, is intimately connected to these individuals, who are for the most part outside the formal structure but who nevertheless command great respect among the mass of Christians.

From his earliest years, he had contact with the finest, as in the holiest, teachers. He did not become a solitary ascetic himself but entered the church. As observed earlier, in letters to civil officials he relates that before he was appointed bishop he lived in a monastery (*Ep.* 80, 81). There is no evidence that he was a priest before being

---

32. As Lane Fox (1997, 217) observes, many saints are born in answer to the prayers of a barren mother. Theodoret is the only individual in the *Religious History* of whom this can be said.

33. Canivet (1977, 45–46) points out that there is evidence of readers being as young as five years old.

made bishop.[34] It is thought that his monastery was in Nicerte, just outside Apamea, because later he referred to "my monastery" (τὸ ἡμέτερον μοναστήριον) when asking to be allowed to go on retreat there after the Council of Ephesus in 449, the Latrocinium (119).

Theodoret was from a wealthy family in the Greek city of Antioch. He and his family, though probably Greek speaking, also understood Syriac, the native tongue of the majority of the population of the area. They and similar high-status individuals (such as the wife of the comes orientis mentioned in *Religious History* 9.5) ventured out of the city occasionally to seek help from holy men in the villages nearby.

Cyrrhus

Theodoret was made bishop of Cyrrhus in 423, apparently against his will (or at least this is what he says). It is customary now to doubt such statements of reluctance as a topos since they occur frequently in the writings of bishops.[35] Presumably it was thought that Christians should not grasp at power, nor should effective leaders have had to do so, and it was much more flattering to have posterity think that high office was thrust upon them.

Cyrrhus was a city in northern Syria, about sixty miles northeast of Antioch in the diocese of Hierapolis. Theodoret, however, mentions Antioch and the bishop there far more often than Hierapolis.[36] Peeters describes Cyrrhus as "une assez misérable petite ville," which gives a picture rather different from Millar's "substantial Greek city."[37] Apart from the fact that Cyrrhus was home to the Legio Fretensis under Tiberius and that it lost its strategic importance after Commagene was reunited with the empire by Vespasian in 72, hardly anything is known about the city before Theodoret wrote about it.[38]

---

34. Ibid., 61.

35. Many instances are listed in Dudley 1991.

36. See Millar 1993, 242; and Naaman 1971, 29–33. Jones as usual is extremely useful; see 1971, 244, 252, 262, 268–69, on Cyrrhus and the surrounding area. See Dalrymple 1997, 159–71, on the place today.

37. Peeters 1950, 66; Millar 1993, 229–30, 236–56. On the area, see also Tchalenko 1953, 1:133–35, 147–49, 205–27.

38. Canivet 1958, 17. In the fourth century, the archaeological finds suggest a significant economic expansion in this area, with bigger and better houses being built (see Tate 1992, 329–32; and Garnsey 1996, 139–42).

From the *Religious History* we know that Cyrrhus had numerous villages in its neighborhood. Unsurprisingly, perhaps, the way Theodoret represented his diocese depended on the audience for which he was writing. In a letter to the prefect Constantius he says that the area of which he was bishop was forty miles long and forty miles across and included many high mountains, some of which were barren while others had scant vegetation. In this letter he was writing on behalf of overtaxed parishioners, and one might expect the picture to be a bleak one in this case (*Ep.* 42). However, when he is complaining to Leo, the bishop of Rome, of the wrongs done him at the council of 449 Theodoret mentions that it had eight hundred churches, which seems to be a remarkably high figure. In this letter he is relating all the hard work he has done in his diocese, so it may not be unreasonable to allow for exaggeration (113). For instance, he reports that there was no heresy or error in the flock of any of these eight hundred churches.

From his account of his activities there it would seem that he spent much time traveling around his diocese, visiting holy men and waging war on heretics. In the same letter to Leo of 449 he protests that during his twenty-six years as bishop he never acquired a house, a plot of land, an obol, or even a tomb but voluntarily embraced poverty, having given up his inheritance on the death of his parents (*Ep.* 113). He did boast elsewhere that he maintained the public baths, and had had porticos, an aqueduct, and two bridges built in Cyrrhus (81).[39] According to letter 83, to Dioscorus, bishop of Alexandria, written in 448, he says that he regularly returned to Antioch to preach. It should be pointed out that he mentions this because he wants to suggest that the bishops of Antioch never thought he was preaching anything heretical. At some point, although we do not know when, he visited Jerusalem.[40]

We know that he was concerned to provide doctors for his community because again he tells us so (*Ep.* 115). He writes letters of recommendation for these individuals when they decide to leave, which they do after he is deposed (114, 115). These documents are also political since he is making the point that the doctors, these assets to Cyrrhus, are leaving because he is also leaving and they were only there because he had the foresight and care to bring them

---

39. Canivet 1977, 62.
40. See *Cure for Hellenic Maladies* (11.71), where he says he saw the desolation of the destruction of the Jewish temple with his own eyes.

in the first place. What is interesting here is that the men in question are not only medical doctors but presbyters. The church was concerned with both body and soul.[41]

The Councils of Ephesus and Chalcedon

It is unclear exactly when Theodoret wrote the *Religious History* except that it was between the councils of Ephesus and Chalcedon.[42] He was caught up in the theological controversies of the day, being involved in the disputes around the Council of Ephesus in 431, which resulted in the deposition, excommunication, and exile of Nestorius, a fellow Antiochene who had been elevated to the most important see of the empire, the imperial capital, Constantinople.[43] Nestorius was the bishop with whom Theodoret's fortunes were most closely tied, and it was later rumored that they were related.[44] In a career strikingly similar to that of John Chrysostom, Nestorius was from Antioch and was appointed bishop of Constantinople in 428.

The main parties in the dispute were the sees of Antioch and Alexandria, and the differences between the two positions are very difficult to discern for the untrained eye. The common characterization is that Antioch's interpretation of the scriptures was literal and precise whereas Alexandria took a more allegorical approach.[45] However, the divergences were not quite so obvious and the position of Cyril, the bishop of Alexandria, was much closer to the Antiochene stance than such a definition allows, as a careful examination of the texts reveals.[46]

Nestorius represented the Antiochene views and, following Diodorus of Tarsus and Theodore of Mopsuestia, supported the objection

41. Adnès and Canivet 1967, 81–82. On the shrine of Cosmas and Damian in Cyrrhus, two Arab doctors who practiced medicine for free, see Peeters 1950, 65–67.

42. There are many accounts of this period. See, for instance, Kidd 1922, 3:193–339; Duchesne 1929, 3:313–88; Devreesse 1945, 48–51; Fliche and Martin 1948, 4:177–86; Downey 1961, 461–66; and Grillmeier 1975, 392–539. See also Young 1991, 70–79; 1983, 268–70.

43. On Nestorius, see Downey 1961, 461–65; Bardy 1948; and entries for Nestorius, Ephesus, and Chalcedon in Bowersock, Brown, and Grabar 1999.

44. Nau (1909, 402–5) dismisses the story that Theodoret was related to Nestorius.

45. See, for instance, Cameron 1993a, 182; or Downey 1961, 461. For a more detailed theological description of the disputes, see Grillmeier 1975, 414–39.

46. See, for example, the reservations in O'Keeffe 2000.

to the use of the term *theotokos* (mother of God) to describe Mary. She was, according to this view, the mother of Christ but not the mother of God. At any rate, this is the view Cyril represented Nestorius as holding. But the latter's position was clearly more sophisticated than that since he had no objection to *theotokos* if it was conjoined with *anthropotokos* (mother of man).[47] Such a distinction offended many, including the empress Pulcheria it seems, and Cyril, the bishop of Alexandria, took advantage of the uproar to organize some opposition to the patriarch. In 430 a council was held in Antioch, which warned Nestorius to be careful in his theological teachings.[48]

Cyril also wrote to the bishop of Rome, Cælestine, who called a council that also condemned Nestorius. Nestorius persuaded the emperor to call another council, and this took place in Ephesus the following year.[49] It hardly seems likely that a council held in a church dedicated to Mary in Ephesus, a city especially venerated as the place where she died, would do anything but condemn such an assault on her dignity, so the place would appear to have been well chosen.[50] However it should be noted that the emperor appointed as his representative, the comes domesticorum, Candidianus, who was a supporter of Nestorius, and it would appear that the imperial intention was to have Nestorius vindicated. The combination of the bishops of Alexandria and Rome, on the other hand, was a powerful one.

In a farcical situation, when the Antiochene party was held up by rain and floods, Cyril and his supporters, such as Memnon of Ephesus and Juvenal of Jerusalem, declared themselves the council and went ahead and deposed Nestorius. Candidianus opposed this action and treated the Syrians as the true council when they arrived. This body then deposed Cyril and Memnon. Legates from the bishop of Rome arrived and sided with Cyril. The emperor, Theodosius, tried

---

47. Chadwick 1951, 149. Chadwick's term *logomachies* describes the impression of the debates for many readers very well (145). On Nestorius, see Grillmeier 1975, 447–63.

48. See Holum 1982, 163, on Pulcheria's role in Nestorius's fall from grace.

49. As Dagron (1970, 262) points out, Gregory of Nazianzus, John Chrysostom, Nestorius, and Flavian, three of them bishops of Constantinople, were all brought down by the combination of the bishop of Alexandria and the monks of Constantinople.

50. For perceptive discussions of the events, see Gregory 1979, 100–116; and Lim 1995, 220–27. Holum (1982, 164) suggests that the choice of Ephesus was to placate Nestorius's enemies, including Pulcheria.

to compromise and confirmed the deposition of Nestorius, Cyril, and Memnon, hoping presumably to get rid of all the arguing parties, but somehow — his enemies said Cyril used bribery and he certainly solicited the help of monks in Constantinople — Cyril and Memnon were restored while Nestorius retired to a monastery.

Theodoret's role during these years is indisputable. He was present at the Council of Ephesus in 431, defending Antiochene views and arguing against the bishop of Alexandria, Cyril.[51] When this ended in conflict, he was invited along as part of the Antiochene party to argue its side against the Egyptians. After the Council Acacius the bishop of Beroea and John of Antioch were invited to Nicomedia to talk to Cyril in an attempt to reach an agreement. John took along as supporters Alexander of Hierapolis and Theodoret. Those on the side of Antioch drew up a short doctrinal document as a basis for agreement that is now known as the Formula of Union. In 433, John accepted the condemnation of Nestorius and entered into communion with the new bishop of Constantinople, Maximian. Theodoret however refused to be part of this although later he did make peace with his opponents without agreeing to condemn Nestorius.[52]

Theodoret's letter of 434 to Alexander, bishop of Hieropolis, is often cited as evidence that local monks put pressure on him to make peace.[53] This document remarks that the comes Titus had written threatening letters not only to Theodoret but to Jacob of Cyrrhestica, Symeon, and Baradatos, monks who are the subjects of lives numbers 21, 26, and 27, respectively, in the *Religious History*.[54] The same

---

51. To modern readers the colorful language of these ancient controversies is perhaps unexpected. In a letter probably dating from 450 Theodoret depicts the Egyptian church as a prostitute who tries to seduce a chaste man (Theodoret) and when she fails calls him an adulterer. On Theodoret's theological importance, see Clayton 1985, 4; and Bergjan 1994, 211–12.

52. For background, see Kidd 1922, 250–65; Azéma 1955, 20–24; Peeters 1950, 94–102; and Leppin 1996a. Chadwick (1951, 147, n. 2) suggests that the Formula of Union was written by Theodoret himself (see also Grillmeier 1975, 433).

53. See, for instance, Grillmeier and Bacht 1953–54, 199–200.

54. Schwartz 1922–23, 170, translated by Festugière (1959, 420–21). Peeters (1950, 98) says that Alexander responded sharply to Theodoret, saying that Macedonius had preached heresy in a church in Daphne. Peeters assumes this is the Macedonius of life 13 of the *Religious History,* but this is improbable for three reasons. First, the name surely is not uncommon. Second, Theodoret's Macedonius probably died about 420 (see Price 1985a, 108, n. 1). Third, Theodoret implies that Macedonius spoke no Greek, so it would seem a little odd that he preached in a church in Daphne. Festugière (1959, 422, 289) does not agree with Peeters's identification either.

three names occur in the Acts of the Council of Chalcedon when the emperor Leo I wrote to them along with eastern bishops in 457. These three monks are the only ones mentioned who were not bishops, but they clearly have very high status in the church.[55] Theodoret says in his letter to Alexander that he was under pressure from Jacob, Symeon, and Baradatus to make peace, but he gives no indication that he will take their advice or that he is much bothered about it. Rather he presents himself as holding out nobly under stress and is prepared to retire to his monastery. The antagonism continued in any case, and in 438 Cyril published three treatises against Diodorus of Tarsus and Theodore of Mopsuestia, two of the leading figures of the Antiochene school.

In 441 John, bishop of Antioch, died. Because Theodoret had refused to condemn Nestorius, relations with John never fully recovered after 433, although they did return to communion when John dropped his requirement that Theodoret condemn Nestorius. The bishop of Antioch was succeeded by his nephew Domnus (who occupied the see from 441–49), with whom Theodoret was on better terms. The other high-profile figures in this episode, Cyril and Proclus, also died. Cyril was succeeded to the see of Alexandria by Dioscorus in 444, and Flavian became bishop of Constantinople in 446. The argument over Nestorianism did not go away, however. Some thought that the Formula of Union of 433 was a capitulation to the supporters of Nestorius. A reconstruction of the exact events of these years is impossible, but clearly hostilities did not cease. Theodoret was seen as a troublemaker and confined to his see in 448 by imperial order (see *Ep.* 79, 80, for his exasperation over this). In the following year, 449, he and the current bishop of Constantinople, Flavian, were deposed at another council at Ephesus. The legitimacy of the council was challenged, and accusations of violence and intimidation were made. Leo, bishop of Rome, dubbed it the Latrocinium, or Robber Council, understandably perhaps, as he himself was excommunicated by Dioscorus.[56]

One of those instrumental in the demise of Theodoret and Flavian was a monk, Eutyches, against whose ideas Theodoret had written

55. Schwartz 1936, 22–24 (for the letter), 23 (for the three names, discussed in Peeters 1950, 101).

56. For a useful résumé of this period, see Bowersock, Brown, and Grabar 1999, 426–27, 369–70. See also Leppin 1996a; and Downey 1961, 467–70.

his *Eranistes,* a work also known as the *Dialogues,* which is thought to have been penned shortly after Cyril's death in 444.[57] In the capital, Constantinople, there was an emergence of new theological ideas, which marked the start of what we know as the monophysite heresy.[58] Eutyches is credited with helping to shape this, and he enjoyed influence with Theodosius II. Unfortunately for both of them the emperor died in 450. His sister Pulcheria, who succeeded him, and her husband disapproved of the methods and results of the recent Council of Ephesus of 449, and in an attempt to impose some order on the unruly clerics called another one in Chalcedon in 451.[59]

This time Flavian was posthumously rehabilitated, Theodoret was reinstated, and the bishop of Alexandria, Dioscorus, was deposed. The canons of the Council of Chalcedon reveal much about the perceived dangers of the period: they are extremely concerned with the role of the monks in church affairs. Monasteries were to submit to the supervision of their local bishops; the movements of lower clergy and monks were restricted, and they were forbidden to plot against their bishops.[60] Chadwick has observed that "Throughout the fourth century the monastic movement was straining to overcome the deep distrust of many of the bishops."[61] By the mid–fifth century it was clear that the monks had failed utterly to dispel the worries of the church hierarchy. The bishops at Chalcedon were openly admitting that they had to exert direct control over these centers of religious zeal. The contrast between these canons and the picture painted by Theodoret in his *Religious History* could not be sharper. Regardless of whether Theodoret was describing the situation in Syria accurately or indulging in wishful thinking, one aspect emerges clearly: the monks were an issue of great consequence to the church.

57. In three dialogues, Theodoret reports the conversation between "Orthodoxos" and his opponent "Eranistes" about theological matters, and, as one might expect, Orthodoxos represents Theodoret's own views. Lim (1991) points out that Theodoret was not the first to include the names of his speakers in the margins (as opposed to the body of the text). Theodoret comments on his practice of doing this in the preface to his work, so presumably it was not common and Theodoret may simply be drawing attention to the fact that he is doing something different from the ancient Greeks and was not concerned with what contemporaries were doing. For Christians it was crucial that the correct views were ascribed to the right names.

58. Downey 1961, 468; Bowersock, Brown, and Grabar 1999, 586–88.

59. Halleux (1993) gives a useful account of the events.

60. This is discussed by Leppin (1996a, 212). See also Dagron 1970, 272–75.

61. Chadwick 1967, 177.

After Theodoret was reinstated we know virtually nothing more about him. It is not even known whether he returned to his see or stayed in the monastery.

Various suggestions have been put forward for his death, such as 457 or 466, but the last certain date for his life is 453 when Leo, the bishop of Rome, wrote to him.[62] His writings against Cyril had the extraordinary honor of being condemned a century after his death at the second Council of Constantinople in 553, along with those of Theodore of Mopsuestia and Ibas of Edessa, when the emperor Justinian was trying to appease the monophysites.[63] This posthumous antagonism reflects his significance in the controversy; Theodoret was crucially important in forming the Christological arguments of the day. Nestorius may have provoked the debate, but others prolonged it, and one of those most actively involved in doing so was Theodoret.[64]

---

62. On the suggested dates, see Azéma 1955 and Honigmann 1953, respectively.

63. Cyril of Scythopolis, who in the sixth century borrows directly from the *Religious History,* omits Theodoret's name from the list of those anathematized at the Council of Chalcedon out of piety toward Theodoret (Binns 1994, 63, 64, 216). This borrowing by Cyril indicates the work's enduring popularity.

64. Clayton 1985, 56. Perhaps rather unkindly, he observes that Theodoret was unable to understand the points Cyril and the Alexandrians were making (519). His argument is that Theodoret's Christology was exactly what the Councils of Ephesus and Chalcedon condemned as Nestorianism (520).

Chapter 2

Writing the *Religious History*

When the church was undergoing great transformations and beginning to take a leading role in the empire's affairs, Theodoret was in
the thick of the activity. His complete writings comprise a huge body
of material. In any introduction to Theodoret, his *Religious History*
is summoned up as witness to his life. It is no impartial testimony to
his virtue, but it can throw some light on his concerns.

The editor of the three volumes of his correspondence, with some
justification, described him as "un des écrivains les plus féconds de
l'Eglise grecque au Ve siècle."[1] The variety of his writings is often
remarked upon, and one suggestion for his motive in writing the
Religious History was that he wanted to try his hand at hagiography
since he had already covered every other ecclesiastical genre, including apologetics, history, exegesis, antiheretical tracts, theology, and
letters.[2] However, there are more serious issues involved in this work
than a mere exercise in genre.

He was clearly conscious of his own output and refers to some of
his works in letters. In letter 82, while protesting his orthodoxy, he
says that people should read those of his works written before and
after the Council of Ephesus. They will see he is not, and never was,
a heretic. He lists his commentaries on the prophets, the psalms,[3]

---

1. Azéma 1955, 9. See also Quasten 1960, 536–54. For a discussion of the dating of
his works, see Richard 1935. On his exegesis, see O'Keeffe 2000 and McCollough 1985,
and on his style see Spadavecchia 1985.

2. Young 1983, 51. Her opinion that "self-defence was not among his intentions"
(52) is stated baldly and without support. See also Jackson [1892] 1994, 14–15. There is a
useful list of his works in Gallico 1995, 32–40.

3. The commentary on the psalms was translated into English for the first time only
in 2000 by Robert Hill (2000).

and the Gospels and says that he wrote against the Arians, Macedonians, Apollinarians, and Marcionites (by which he is referring to the *Dialogues* or *Eranistes*). In addition he had written on the Mysteries, Providence, the questions of the magi, the lives of the saints (referring to the *Religious History*), and much more. Similarly, in his letter to Leo (*Epistle* 113) he says that he possesses the works he has written over the past twenty years which all show his orthodoxy: works arguing against the Arians, Eunomians, Jews, pagans (the *Cure for Hellenic Maladies*), and the magi of Persia; works on Providence, theology, and the divine incarnation; and commentaries on the Gospels and the prophets. In letter 116 of 449 he gives much the same list, although he adds the detail that he wrote more than thirty books inveighing against the usual offenders, Arians, Eunomians, Marcionites, Macedonians, pagans, and Jews. In the same vein he gives a comparable list to the monks of Constantinople in 451, although he disarmingly opens the paragraph following this list with the words "And what need is there of many words, when it is possible to refute falsehood in few?"[4]

The work most frequently consulted by historians today is his *Ecclesiastical History,* which covers approximately the same period as those by Socrates and Sozomen, that is, from Constantine to the early fifth century.[5] Theodoret's covers the shortest period of the three since there is very little about the reign of Theodosius II, who came to the throne in 408, in the last book.[6] Virtually the only episode that concerns his reign is the return in 438 of the remains of John Chrysostom, another important son of Antioch. Sozomen's history ends in 425 and Socrates' in 439. Theodoret's history is markedly different from the other two, being much more outspoken in its condemnation of those he considered enemies.[7] The emperor Julian,

---

4. This is *Epistle* 145 in the *Nicene and Post-Nicene Fathers* translation but *Epistle* 146 in the *Sources Chrétiennes* edition (Azéma 1955–65).

5. For a succinct description of Theodoret's history, see Chesnut 1986, 207–14. For a comparison with those of Socrates and Sozomen, see Leppin 1996b. We do not know exactly when any of the histories were written (discussed Urbainczyk 1997b).

6. The work is divided into five books, whereas those of Socrates and Sozomen were seven and nine, respectively.

7. Barnes (1993, 209) remarks about Theodoret that "he transformed the raw materials of his *Ecclesiastical History* to suit his own purposes more thoroughly than either Socrates or Sozomen." One might wish to argue that it is easier to see Theodoret's purpose since his attitudes are obviously those of a bishop. Momigliano comments about Theo-

for instance, is described in the blackest terms, with no redeeming features. One might interpret this black and white representation as having been due to Theodoret's position within the church, that is, as a bishop actively involved in the controversies, whereas Sozomen and Socrates were both laymen.[8] Theodoret also places much more emphasis on Antioch in his church history, especially in the final book, which paints a much starker picture of the treatment of John Chrysostom. Only in Theodoret's history do we see Theodosius II weeping for the sins of his parents over the remains of John Chrysostom (*Ecclesiastical History* 5.36).

Perhaps one of the episodes that best illustrates the differences between the three historians is the interchange between Ambrose, bishop of Milan, and the emperor Theodosius I after the massacre of Thessalonica. Theodoret reports that seven thousand were killed in Thessalonica (Theodosius had had the population of the city executed for lynching for *magister militum*). Socrates simply omits all mention of it. Sozomen describes it in ways that reflect well on the bishop but only briefly (Sozomen, *Ecclesiastical History* 7.25). Theodoret milks it for all it's worth, giving Ambrose very forthright and long denunciations of the emperor, for example, "Your coming is the coming of a tyrant. You are raging against God. You are trampling on his laws" (5.17 = 5.18 of the Greek text).[9] In turn, the emperor weeps for eight months, grovels on the floor, tears out his hair, and bangs his head on the ground in repentance and misery. Ambrose eventually allows him into the church but keeps him out of the innermost part, telling him that this is reserved for priests and that "Purple can make emperors but not priests."[10] Theodoret finds both bishop and emperor commendable, the bishop for his outspokenness (παρρησία) and the emperor for his obedience (εὐπάθεια).

The last event in Theodoret's history is the record of the death of

doret that "He maintains an ominous silence on the Nestorian dispute of which he was one of the protagonists, but is otherwise outspoken, even brutal in his partisan judgments (1990, 143).

    8. Urbainczyk 1997a, 13–14. On the differences between Socrates and Sozomen, see Urbainczyk 1997b.

    9. The most recent Greek edition is in the Die Griechischen christlichen Schriftsteller series, edited Leon Parmentier (1998).

    10. Sozomen also describes Ambrose as putting the emperor literally in his place in the church (discussed Urbainczyk 1997b, 361). See also Leppin on Theodosius I (1996b, 105–21).

Theodore of Mopsuestia, a very important figure for Antiochene theology. Crucial for understanding Theodoret's thoughts are the remarks he makes just before this event, at virtually the end of the history:

> These wars [against pagans] and the victory of the church had been predicted by the Lord, and the event teaches us that war brings us more blessing than peace. Peace makes us delicate, easy and cowardly. War whets our courage and makes us despise this present world as passing away. But these are observations which we have often made in other writings. (Theodoret, *Ecclesiastical History* 5.38 = Greek text 5.39)

Theodoret was not interested in peace at any price, and these bellicose words indicate very forcefully the differences between him and the other two historians. They also help to explain his presence in the arguments of his day and, I would argue, confirms the idea that the *Religious History* is part of a struggle, not the product of a quiet hour.[11]

The *Religious History*

Theodoret's *Religious History* is, in spite of its title, a series of lives of Syrian holy men. However it is more than simply an account of their lives. As I will argue, it places Syria, the church, and last but not at all least Theodoret at the heart of this piece of hagiography. This is not accidental. The background to the work was the period between the Councils of Ephesus and Chalcedon, a time of monumental struggle between the two schools of theology represented by Antioch and Alexandria, which was of great consequence to both sides and was partly conducted by monks. It seems most improbable that Theodoret took time off from this controversy or took advantage of a lull in it to write a minor piece about local friends. The exact date of the composition of the work is impossible to establish. We can safely say that it was written before the *Ecclesiastical History* because he refers to his earlier work in that one. Arguments have

---

11. In this I am in agreement with Leppin 1996a.

been put forward for a range of dates in the 440s, in which there was no major council until 449. This is partly why it has been assumed that Theodoret had a relatively quiet time and took advantage of it to write this piece praising his friends. However, the fact that there was a very tumultuous council in 449 surely points to the preceding years as ones fraught with maneuvering.[12] This work is a serious political tract, which demonstrates Syria's importance in producing holy men, the church's importance in mediating with them, and Theodoret's unique position as a local bishop who has known some of these remarkable, holy, and miracle-working individuals all his life.[13] The implication is that any fight against the Syrian church and Theodoret also means a fight against these men of God.

The label *Religious History* is rather misleading. It developed from a literal translation of the Latin title, *Historia Religiosa,* which in turn is from *philotheos historia* (φιλόθεος ἱστορία), a description Theodoret himself uses in the prologue to describe his work. In the same passage he says that readers can call it what they like and offers the alternative "an ascetic life" (ἀσκητικὴ πολιτεία, Prologue 10).[14] In a letter he calls his opus "lives of holy men" (τῶν ἁγίων οἱ βίοι, *Epistle* 82), but it is known now as the *Religious History.* In the life of Abraham (*Religious History* 17.11) he calls his work a history of

12. Canivet (1977, 32–33) favors 444, while Price (1985a, xiii–xv) suggests 440 (but see Leppin 1996a, 213, n. 3). Peeters (1950, 96) argues that Theodoret wrote the work while under stress. Leppin (1996a) takes this up again, and in essence I agree, although my argument does not depend on a historical reconstruction of events but looks at the internal evidence.

13. Peeters's argument (1950, 100) that Theodoret wrote the *Religious History* to get back into favor with the monks is contradicted by the work itself, as I will show throughout the book. It is true, however, that the historical background of the disputes between the Antiochene and Alexandrian churches shapes the text. It is also true that he wants to make clear to his readers that he and the Antiochene clerics have a good and uncomplicated relationship with the local monks (see Leppin 1996a, 214).

14. The work is often referred to as *L'Histoire Philothée.* In *On Divine Love* (15) we see the importance of the term *philotheos* (ὁ τοίνυν τῷ ὄντι φιλόσοφος καὶ φιλόθεος ἂν εἰκότως καλοῖτο "therefore the true philosopher [friend of wisdom] could appropriately be called friend of God"; Price's translation [1985a, 200]). The word πολιτεία can mean "way of life" as well as the more usual "citizenship" or "government" (see Liddell and Scott 1968 and Lampe 1961). For example, in *Religious History* 9.8 he uses the verb πολιτεύω to describe his mother living according to Peter's rules. Cf. Socrates' *Ecclesiastical History* (4.23), which gives alternative titles for works by Evagrius. See also *Religious History* 17.1, where Theodoret uses both terms, *politeia* and *bios,* with *politeia* meaning "profession" and *bios* meaning "way of life." So, although Abraham changed his *politeia,* he did not change his ascetic *bios.*

monks (τῶν μοναχῶν ἱστορία). The word ἱστορία can mean "inquiry," "information," or even "story" or "narrative," so it is rather broader than our term *history*.

It is customary to make a sharp distinction between biography and history, so it is salutary to notice Theodoret's more relaxed approach to labeling his work. If one takes history to mean a narration of the past, in some sense biography is history. Just as his *Ecclesiastical History* is a narration of events of the church, so this work is a narration of piety, of pious individuals.[15] Canivet and Leroy-Molinghen call their edition *Histoire des Moines de Syrie,* which Price follows for his translation *A History of the Monks of Syria.* This is a neat parallel to the *History of the Monks of Egypt,* although it is a little misleading about the contents of the text. Canivet and Leroy-Molinghen point out that it could not legitimately be called a history of monasticism since the work gives a short account of one individual after another rather than any discussion of the development of the phenomenon of monasticism or the communities involved.[16] For the same reason *A History of the Monks of Syria* is not a wholly satisfactory designation. Theodoret's own alternative, "lives of holy men," or τῶν ἁγίων οἱ βίοι (*Epistle* 82), is perhaps the most accurate.

The accounts of the monks are of varying length, the longest being that of Jacob of Cyrrhestica at thirty-five paragraphs and the shortest that of Salamanes, which is a mere three.[17] They all describe males apart from three women who are mentioned briefly at the end. The work conventionally is divided into thirty chapters, although it has been shown convincingly that it was written in twenty-eight (two, numbers 22–23 and 24–25, were wrongly separated at some point).[18] However, as all other works and the edition and translations refer to the lives as if there were thirty, it seems less confusing to use the numbering employed by everyone else. Usually each account is concerned with one individual, although occasionally one deals with

---

15. By the time Theodoret wrote the *Ecclesiastical History* he only refers to the work as *philotheos historia.* References in the translation of the *Ecclesiastical History* to the *Religious History* are 1.6.4, 2.26.3, 3.19.1, 4.22.5, and 4.24.2. Because of a different numbering of the chapters, the references in Parmentier's Greek text are 1.7.4, 2.30.3, 3.24.1, 4.25.5, and 4.27.2. See Canivet 1977, 79–82, on the title.

16. Canivet and Leroy-Molinghen 1977, 41.

17. These comprise twenty-nine pages of Greek and two pages, respectively, in the *Sources Chrétiennes.*

18. Devos 1979.

more, for instance, the last two, which concern the sisters Marana and Cyra.[19]

Generally, the reader learns where the holy men and women came from and sometimes a little about their background followed by a description of how they lived and what they did, which normally takes the form of a series of anecdotes. These would naturally contain aspects of asceticism: activities like starving themselves, exposing themselves to extremes of heat and cold, and the wearing of chains.[20] The denial of sexual desire, although it occurs in other works of this genre, does not play a large role in the *Religious History*.[21] Often we see the ascetic's relationship with others such as locals, governors, bishops, emperors, and Theodoret. Some performed miracles, the most common being ones of healing and exorcism.[22] Finally, but importantly, Theodoret frequently gives details of their pupils, individuals coming to learn from these masters who sometimes formed communities around or near them.[23]

The structure is neither odd nor complicated, although the description can make it appear so.[24] Theodoret is following the chronology of his own life since he was from Antioch and grew up there before being made bishop of Cyrrhus. Thus, the first ascetics he writes about are from Antioch and the more recent from Cyrrhus. Some of those he knew, or knew of, from his childhood would be dead; the ones he met later would still be living.[25] Theodoret does not explain that this is what he is doing. It may be that the structure was so obvious to him that he did not feel the need to explain it. Whether consciously or not, the work is centered around Theodoret. He forms the core of it,

19. One can see how the error of splitting the chapters came about, though, as these two (22–23, 24–25) are different in that they concern more than one individual, three in these cases, and all the rest of the lives are only about one individual, apart from the chapter on Marana and Cyra.

20. See *Religious History* 27.1, wherein he gives a description of all the different forms of asceticism he has mentioned.

21. Cf., for example, *Lausiac History* 3, 5, 8, 28, 29; and *History of the Monks of Egypt* 1.32–35, 16, 20, 24.

22. On this, see Canivet 1977, 117–45, which largely reproduces the conclusions of Adnès and Canivet 1967.

23. On this aspect of teaching, see Rousseau 1997, 1998.

24. See, for instance, the descriptions in Canivet 1977, 83–86, Festugière 1959, 426–47; and Price 1985a, xvi–xvii.

25. David Buck (1976, 292–307) has argued convincingly that Palladius also structured his *Lausiac History* on an autobiographical framework. See also Hunt 1973 on the *Lausiac History* and its autobiographical content.

and this is not fortuitous. Nor is the large amount of information we receive about him. It would appear that "Theodoret's inclusion of personal reminiscences of his own contacts with Syrian monks over the whole course of his life" is more than simply "one of the most delightful features of the *Religious History*."[26]

Theodoret begins with figures from the more distant past, and the earlier lives reflect the longer tradition behind the stories. Theodoret himself draws attention to the structure of his work as he writes, although he does not elucidate it in his prologue or even allude to any plan for its composition. Perhaps surprisingly, he does not reveal the geographic location of his subjects except in the body of the work. His first ascetic is Jacob of Nisibis, and the second, Julian Saba, was also from Mesopotamia, but Julian travels and the life ends with an anecdote based in Cyrrhus, a place of crucial importance in the *Religious History* since Theodoret was its bishop.[27] The third holy man is Marcianus, a native of Cyrrhus, who went to live in the desert.[28]

Theodoret introduces the fourth life, that of Eusebius of Teleda, saying that paragons of virtue can also flourish in human society, but he seems to forget his first example, Jacob, who was in fact bishop of Nisibis. One thing the first three do have in common is that they are all explicitly said to be anti-Arian. They actively help in the struggle against Arianism, and I would argue that this is another, perhaps more important, reason why Theodoret included them. There was a famous precedent for this in the *Life of Antony*, a large part of which focuses on this aspect of his activities. The reader of the *Religious History* is shown that Syria as well as Egypt has a tradition of militant holy men.[29] Theodoret places his holy men in a venerable line of such individuals by relating this activity, and he is also able to illustrate that holy men are powerful allies for their bishops. These remarkable

---

26. Price 1985a, xi.

27. See Peeters 1920 on Theodoret's account of Jacob of Nisibis.

28. Rousseau suggests that the first three holy men are located in the desert so that Theodoret can make the point that one can find them elsewhere as well: "The first three stories of the *HR*, privileging the desert, were designed only to prepare for the admission that ascetic virtues could flourish elsewhere; the 'built-up area' was not inimical to 'philosophy'" (1998, 240).

29. He was not the first to celebrate Syrian holy men. Jerome had written the life of Malchus, who was also from the area around Antioch. Carolinne White (1998) has provided a very useful set of translations of Jerome's lives of Malchus, Paul of Thebes, and Hilarion, as well as the lives of Antony, Martin of Tours, and Benedict. Quotations of these works are her translation unless otherwise noted.

individuals can and will help in the fight against heresy, alongside their bishops. It should not be forgotten that in the arguments between the Alexandrians and Antiochenes after Ephesus both sides (naturally enough perhaps) called each other heretics.

The issue of the city-desert dichotomy has been discussed extensively, and perhaps what is most significant in Theodoret's case is that it is relatively unimportant. The contrast is not so much in the spatial separation as the participation or nonparticipation of the holy man in society. Goehring has argued that the desert-city contrast is a literary metaphor that predated holy men and that it was when the latter fitted the model — that is, by leaving the city for the desert — that literature began to be written about them. This provocative suggestion leads very nicely to his final statement, that "the literary icon conquered history," but it leaves much open to question.[30] There is also an inbuilt inconsistency here in that Goehring is able to construct this argument *from* literary evidence so therefore he must have received information that does not conform to the metaphor. That is, we know from literature that not all monks withdrew to the desert. The comment in the *Life of Antony* that the desert was made a city is emphasizing the new society, remarking on the numbers of those who had made a decision to take up a different life outside regular society by using an oxymoron.

This surely is the initiative behind the literature, that is, the desire to explain the new and more desirable way of life being chosen by some individuals. The idea that people wrote because they saw a situation that fit a metaphor is questionable. It seems rather more plausible to think that the metaphor was used because it was apt and that authors had more profound reasons for going to the lengths of writing a book than merely to use a metaphor. It is more probable that people wrote such accounts *because* monks began going to the desert. That is, these individuals were leaving society, so how would that society know about them if they were no longer in its midst? The answer was to preserve their memory and hold up their example by writing about them, which is, after all, what most of the authors inform us they are doing. Spatial separation may have been crucial in the development of this literature, but surely this was for practical not aesthetic or literary reasons.[31] It could also be that literature

---

30. Goehring 1993, 296.

31. See Griffith 1995; and Elm 1994, 283–84, on the problems of knowing about Syrian and female asceticism, respectively.

encourages would-be ascetics to live in the desert, as their presence in the city is too dangerous to the established church.[32]

At the opening of the fourteenth life, that of Maësymas, Theodoret comments that he will now describe the holy men who lived in the region of Cyrrhus and explains retrospectively that the first thirteen had come from the area around Antioch.[33] He says that he realizes there were others who could have been included but he will now move on to Cyrrhus. When we reach the twenty-first life, Theodoret explains that the first twenty men were dead and he will now describe those still living. He draws attention to the fact that he had begun the whole work with a man called Jacob and was making another, Jacob of Cyrrhestica, the first of the living. The lives of the living are generally shorter than those of the deceased, perhaps because there had been more time for stories to build up around them or because it was more important to establish the accounts of those who were dead.

However, there are significant exceptions to this general pattern: the two longest lives of the whole work are those of living ascetics, Jacob of Cyrrhestica (*Religious History* 21) and Symeon Stylites (26).[34] Symeon was already widely known throughout the empire by the time Theodoret wrote about him, and Devos speculates that Theodoret's original intention was to culminate with him and that the rest are merely afterthoughts.[35] It is certainly true that the final four lives are not substantial. Theodoret stresses Symeon's celebrity status in his life, telling his readers that he was revered even in Rome and the western empire (26.11). He also explicitly comments on Symeon's fight against paganism, Jews, and heretics (26.27). Whether significantly or not, he does not mention Egypt as a place that shows respect for his star ascetic.[36]

Canivet has counted seventy-five ascetics referred to in the *Religious History,* and in the majority of cases this is the only reference to them.[37] So without Theodoret's work most of these persons would be forgotten. One can therefore begin to appreciate the importance of

---

32. This develops a suggestion made by Elm (1994, 383).

33. See Wilson 1983, 32, on the importance of saints for the prestige of their dioceses.

34. The description of his death is a later addition.

35. Devos 1979, 334–35.

36. Rome had often been an ally of the Antiochenes against the church in Egypt (Dagron 1970).

37. Canivet 1977, 83.

Theodoret's work for any discussion of Syrian monasticism. Theodoret was classically educated and wrote in Greek, and his work portrays these holy men through a Hellenistic filter.[38] It could be argued that our whole view of Syrian asceticism is warped because we rely on nonnative accounts that do not understand their subjects, that is, the Greek texts of Theodoret, Palladius, and Sozomen.[39] It has also been observed that some of the Syriac texts that have usually been attributed to Ephraim, and therefore used as a source for early Syrian asceticism, are in fact from a later period.[40] Consequently, we know very little about this subject.

Egyptian monasticism, on the other hand, was celebrated by a series of relatively early works, starting with the *Life of Antony* (composed about 357), *The History of the Monks of Egypt* (dated to approximately 400), and Palladius's *Lausiac History* (dated to 419–420).[41] They were immediately influential pieces of writing and were copied, translated, and widely circulated. Their importance for Theodoret's own composition will be examined next. The *Religious History,* then, is not a history of religion or a pious tract but a collection of lives of Syrian holy men arranged chronologically, with the first thirteen describing those around Antioch and the rest those from Cyrrhus and its environs, following Theodoret's own migration. The author appears as a child with his mother in the early lives and as a bishop in the later ones. There are important similarities and even more significant differences between the work Theodoret wrote and collections about Egyptian monks that he probably knew about. The next chapter will set his text in context.

---

38. Goehring 1992, 248.

39. Griffith 1995, 220–21.

40. Griffith 1995. On the *Liber Graduum* as an expression of the Syrian mentality, see Griffith 1995, 222; and Wickham 1993.

41. See Quasten 1960, 39–45, 176–80, esp. 177–79. On the authorship of the *Life of Antony,* see Barnes 1986; 1993, 240, n. 64. See Van Uytfanghe 1993 for a discussion of hagiography. It does not seem that the *Religious History* was meant for a Syriac-speaking audience, not only because of the obvious fact that the work is in Greek but because, of the Syriac fragments remaining, there are only translations of certain lives, those of Jacob of Nisibis, Julian Saba, Abraham of Carrhae, and Symeon Stylites (see Canivet and Leroy-Molinghen 1977, 60–62). See also the discussion in Drijvers 1981 of the Syriac flavor of Theodoret's lives. Interestingly, there is a twelfth-century manuscript of an Arabic translation of some of the *Religious History,* that is, the lives of Maron, Jacob of Cyrrhestica, Symeon Stylites, Marana and Cyra, and Palladius (Canivet and Leroy-Molinghen 1977, 63).

Chapter 3

Other Lives:
The Literary Background

Theodoret was not the first to write about the lives of holy men, but his book was different from previous examples. He eschewed demons, disease, and disconcertingly attractive women, real or illusionary. His monks were not proud or sinful but remained resolutely virtuous. His text was also more difficult to read, having been written in a learned, classical style replete with athletic metaphors and classical vocabulary. The difference in style reflects a difference in circumstances rather than Theodoret's more educated tastes. He wrote at a time when he had everything to gain and everything to lose. He could not afford to pander to entertainment or include wildly improbable but fascinating anecdotes like those in the other works discussed in this chapter. The Syrian ascendancy in the capital was on the wane, and Theodoret's position was under threat. The *Religious History* reflects the exigencies of the time.

Related Works

When Theodoret wrote the *Religious History*, other works that bore a striking resemblance to his were in circulation. They are similar in being lives of holy men; one might be tempted to call them hagiography, but there is more in common between them than mere glorification of an individual. They relate the lives of individuals who have decided to leave society and live either by themselves or in communities with like-minded people. They have chosen to withdraw because they wish to live holier lives than is possible in normal circumstances and thus devote themselves to lives of prayer and self-denial, with a view toward benefits superior to material comfort. These earlier works celebrate monks of Egypt for the most part and are better known than Theodoret's *Religious History,* partly because they are written in a livelier and more accessible style and partly because the information on Egyptian monasticism is so much more plentiful for this period. In what follows I wish to draw attention to those aspects Theodoret chose to repeat in his own work and those he chose to ignore, since he clearly had them in mind when writing his own.

Christian biography was not merely a description but implicitly also acted as a prescription for how people should live. The subjects of biography were models being held up for others to follow.[1] Classical biography in some sense had also served this purpose, and Plutarch's moralizing *Lives* always found an appreciative audience among Christian readers for this reason.[2] There are similarities between the classical biography and Christian material as early as the Gospels as well as in later texts.[3] However while classical biography often included the subject's faults, these became less common in the Christian material. It is interesting to note that as biography became more popular after Constantine, because of its adoption by Christians, pagans also turned to it.[4]

Porphyry's *Life of Plotinus* is worth considering in this context since the author, like Theodoret, plays a very prominent role in his work, even repeating his own name incessantly as if the reader might forget it.[5] The image of a philosopher is conventionally more eccentric than that of a bishop, so the life is entertaining in a different way. For instance, we would not find Theodoret reporting a story about himself such as the one where Porphyry reads out such an obscure

---

1. See Swain 1997, 33; and Cameron 1991, 141–54, on the importance of biography for Christianity.

2. See Duff 1999, 3–5, on the phenomenal influence of Plutarch on later writers.

3. Most recently, see Hägg and Rousseau (2000b) on these relationships. See also Cox 1983, 3–4.

4. See Momigliano 1971, 9, on the importance of biography after the time of Constantine. See Cameron 1991, 145, on the apparent war of biographies between Christians and neo-Platonists.

5. See Clark 2000 on aspects of this life. Brown (1980) challenges the comparison between pagan philosophers and Christian ascetics, arguing that the former operated within society while the latter were removing themselves from it. See Wimbush 1986 for a discussion of these ideas.

poem that someone in the company says "Porphyry is mad." It is true that the author clearly thinks that he has gone on to show how wrong this comment was, but nevertheless the seed of suspicion is planted in the reader's mind (*Life of Plotinus* 15). We generally find out no slightly disturbing particulars about the ascetics in the *Religious History* such as the fact that Plotinus used to go to his nurse and bare her breast in order to suck it until he was eight years old (3).

Hagiography is not a literary genre but can be present in a wide range of different types of texts, such as sermons, hymns, and letters, as well as biographies.[6] Its purpose is celebration and edification.[7] Theodoret's *Religious History* clearly falls into this category. He says explicitly throughout the work that this is his purpose, as do the authors of the Egyptian works. If one labels this type of writing as biography, then scholars have been keen to draw distinctions within the genre.[8] Patricia Cox examined the lives of philosophers and their relationship with the lives of holy men, arguing that we can discern two types, the lives of sons of gods and those of godlike individuals.[9] She points out that sons of gods have birth stories and perform miracles, whereas godlike subjects have no birth stories and perform no miracles. Interesting from the point of view of the *Religious History* is the fact that, while several of the holy men perform miracles, none has a birth story except the author himself.[10]

By the time Theodoret was writing in the 440s, Jerome had already written his lives of Malchus and Hilarion and Sulpicius Severus his of Martin of Tours, but it is impossible to say whether Theodoret knew these Latin works and it would seem he did not know Latin.[11] It is difficult to determine how widely Latin works were read in the east

---

6. Van Uytfanghe 1993, 146. See also Krueger 1996, 36–56, on the main features of late antique hagiography and on the Gospels as a model for it (108). Burridge (1992, 26–54, esp. 53) defends the study of genre as essential to an understanding of a text, arguing that genre creates expectations in the readers and that one needs to know what these are to understand how the text was interpreted by its audience. While this is true, it is also the case that genre was much more fluid than modern scholars would like, hence Burridge's long chapter on the matter and how, when we try to categorize texts too rigidly, we create new problems.

7. Elliott 1987, 3.

8. For a clear discussion of the problems of genre with regard to the *Vita Constantini,* see Cameron 1997.

9. Cox 1983, 30–36.

10. See later discussions of miracles, and Theodoret's birth, in chapters 7 and 11.

11. See chapter 2 and *Cure for Hellenic Maladies* 5.74.

anyway, although Socrates claimed to have used Rufinus's history (Socrates, *Ecclesiastical History* 2.1).[12] Sozomen mentions Hilarion visiting Antony, but this is no indication that he knew Jerome's work (Sozomen, *Ecclesiastical History* 3.14).

It should be remembered that there would have been other lives circulating that are no longer extant, for instance, those mentioned by Socrates such as *The Monk* by Evagrius and the life of Eusebius Emisenus by George of Laodicea (Socrates, *Ecclesiastical History* 4.23, 1.24, 2.9.2).[13] At the end of his chapter on Egyptian monks Socrates refers readers to Palladius if they wish to learn more (4.23); Sozomen, less specifically, after writing about various monks tells his readers to read their lives if they want further information, giving no details about authors (Sozomen, *Ecclesiastical History* 1.14). Sozomen mentions monks far more often in his church history than Socrates or Theodoret do in theirs, devoting seven chapters of book 6 to the monks of Egypt, Syria, and Palestine (6.28–34). It is very likely that he was able to consult written lives for many of these. In other words, there was a considerable body of literature circulating that celebrated the lives of monks and ascetics.

The *Life of Antony* is often described as the model for all subsequent lives of holy men, but few imitated it very closely. It is reasonable to assume that Theodoret knew this highly influential work. Ascribed to the bishop Athanasius, it is thought to have been written in 357.[14] Interestingly, Socrates, who mentions Antony only twice, refers to the *Life of Antony* in both cases and informs us that it was

12. See Urbainczyk 1997a, 51–52, on Socrates' use of Rufinus. It has been suggested that he was actually using the Greek history of Gelasius of Caesarea. Whatever the probability of this suggestion, what is interesting is that Socrates is at least making the claim that he has used a Latin text. He would not have done so if he had no access to one.

13. Also interesting in the respect of Theodoret's *Religious History* is that Socrates gives alternative titles for two of Evagrius's works, *The Monk*, which was also known as *On Active Virtue*, and *The Gnostic*, which is also referred to as *To One Who Is Deemed Worthy of Knowledge* (Socrates, *Ecclesiastical History* 4.23). Socrates, at 7.17, says that Chrysanthus, bishop of the Novatians, was the kind of person Evagrius says monks in the desert should be. The case of Eusebius Emisenus is interesting when it is considered in conjunction with Theodoret's career. Eusebius was from Edessa and went to Antioch but was appointed to the see of Alexandria by the bishop of Constantinople. He went instead to Emisa because of the hostility of the Alexandrians, who were loyal to Athanasius, but he was no more popular there so he went to Laodicea. The life was clearly a favorable one since Socrates tells us that George gives details of his miracles. Hansen (1995) reads "encomium" at Socrates, *Ecclesiastical History* 2.9.2.

14. See Barnes 1986; 1993, 240, n. 64, on the authorship of this work.

written by Athanasius, whereas Sozomen, who mentions Antony much more often, never refers to the *Life* or its author (Sozomen, *Ecclesiastical History* 1.13, 1.14, 3.13, 3.14, 3.15, 6.5, 6.33), even when he is relating the close connection between Antony and Athanasius (2.17, 2.31). It could be that Sozomen did not think that Athanasius wrote the life, but he never indicates that he knows this particular text. Theodoret in his *Ecclesiastical History* mentions Antony only twice, very briefly, and does not mention Athanasius's *Life* (Theodoret, *Ecclesiastical History* 4.18 = 4.21.6 in Greek, 4.24 = 4.27.1 in Greek). He does not mention any similar works in the *Religious History.*

The *Life of Antony* quickly became extremely popular and succeeded in glorifying and immortalizing Antony so that he is remembered as the founder of monastic activity, even though the text itself bears witness to the presence of monks before Antony embarked on his career.[15] As Goehring points out, "The image of Antony as the father of monasticism is dependent less on the historical undertaking of Antony than on the literary success of the *Life of Antony.*"[16] As one might expect there are echoes of the *Life of Antony* in Theodoret's work. The writer of the *Life,* whether it was Athanasius or somebody else, says that he, as the author, will benefit from the narrative and holds Antony up as a model for others. There is an emphasis on how famous Antony is already (93), which is echoed in Theodoret's comments in the life of Symeon (*Religious History* 26.1, 11, 13). Antony performs miracles and exorcisms, has connections with wealthy people who turn to him for help, is held in honor by the imperial court, and has a great respect for clergy, joining them in fighting heresy (*Life of Antony* 80, 15, 61, 67, 81, 69).

The most obvious difference between Theodoret's *Religious History* and the *Life of Antony* is that the latter is extremely long, much

---

15. See Rousseau 1978, 249–50, on the Greek and Latin versions of the *Life of Antony.*

16. Goehring 1992, 239. Jerome, of course, did not make this mistake when he wrote the life of Paul of Thebes, who was senior to Antony. Rousseau (1978, 133) suggests that Jerome wished to rival the achievements of Athanasius and wrote the life of Paul of Thebes to prove that Antony was not the first ascetic in Egypt. See also Rousseau 1978, 143–51, on Sulpicius Severus's writing to show that Antony was not the sole exemplar of the ascetic life. See also O'Neill 1989, which argues convincingly that Christianity always had monasticism as a continuation of its Jewish roots and suggests that some Jewish monasteries simply converted to Christianity.

longer than any of the constituent lives of the *Religious History.* The huge amount of direct speech attributed to Antony is also a feature very rarely found in other saints' lives. This didactic speech is composed of advice to monks (we are told it was in Coptic) and represents a large proportion of the text (chapters 16–43). There is no equivalent in Theodoret's work.

Antony was from a noble Christian family from Egypt, and when his parents died he gave away his substantial property (*Life of Antony* 1–2). Despite his status, he refused to read or write or play and instead stayed at home or went to church.[17] Antony's popularity is emphasized throughout, and we are told that he was loved by everyone (4). The devil is present with temptations in every conceivable form (5), whereas Theodoret denies him any significant role in his work. Antony's appearance is also described several times, and he looks fit and healthy. This is commented on because one might not have expected this, given the deprivations of his life (67). The author also gives a physical description of him at the end of the work rather in the style of classical biography.[18] In contrast, Theodoret rarely mentions the ascetic's appearance, which certainly does not have the importance found in the Egyptian work. Washing and cleanliness are not concerns of Theodoret, whereas the first two principal virtues of Antony were that he did not change his clothes or wash his feet (93).

The similarities between the *History of the Monk of Egypt,* which was composed in approximately 440, and Theodoret's work are much more pronounced.[19] The *History of the Monks of Egypt* is the same type of work, being for the most part a series of lives of holy men. There are twenty-six chapters. It has usually been seen as a series of vignettes of monks, an inspiration to piety given authority

17. Rubenson (2000, 115) comments that Antony's rejection of education was a sign of his inherent holiness. He does not undergo transformation but rejects change in order to remain holy.

18. See Pseudo-Aristotle's *Physiognomics* (English translation by W.S. Hett in *Aristotle: Minor Works,* Loeb Classical Library, Cambridge, Mass., vol. 14, 1936, 83–137); Evans 1969, esp. 46–58; and Barton 1994, 95–131, on an earlier period. See also Frank 2000, 134–70, on the importance of physical appearance in the works of early Christian writers.

19. See the useful description in Young 1983, 38–39. See Bammel 1996 on the relationship between the Greek and Latin versions of the *History of the Monks of Egypt,* especially 97–104. Bammel suggests that the Greek version we possess, which is clearly not the same as the one Rufinus had in front of him when he made his translation, has been clumsily revised by an anti-Origenist.

by the first-person narrative, an eyewitness account. Recently it has been argued that this work is a piece of travel writing.[20] It is true that it relates a journey made by someone 'who is not from the area and describes places and individuals to people who also are not native to the place. While it is useful to be reminded that it may have acted as a guide for future pilgrims, it is less clear how helpful a narrow focus on this particular function is.[21] Theodoret was no outsider in Syria; indeed, his work is designed specifically to emphasize his insider nature. There was no obvious journey since he came from Antioch and later worked in Cyrrhus. Nevertheless, it is true that, like the *History of the Monks of Egypt,* the work was structured around his own geographical movements.[22]

Both the *History of the Monks of Egypt* and the *Religious History* are collections of biographies. Patricia Cox Miller has recently discussed the implications of this, drawing attention to the similarities among the lives in the collection: "When the principle of organization generates objects that are 'the same' — whether they are philosophers, sophists or politicians — there is a simultaneous drive to show how they are different."[23] She observes that the *History of the Monks of Egypt* was the first collective biography of which we are aware that was written in Greek by a Christian. There are previous pagan examples, most notably Plutarch's *Parallel Lives.* One might observe that the *History of the Monks of Egypt*'s emphasis is on the sheer numbers of monks, and in this case a collection makes the point most effectively. Despite the less exaggerated number of Syrian holy men presented by Theodoret, his concern is to describe the area in which he lived as studded with ascetic stars. The *Religious History,* like the *History of the Monks of Egypt,* is a collection of lives, describing

---

20. Frank 1998, 2000. Fowden (1999, 93) also refers to the *History of the Monks of Egypt* and *Lausiac History* as travelogues. Rousseau (1978, 221) describes Cassian's work as written to provide an armchair pilgrimage for readers. Earlier (79–91) he draws attention to the importance of travel for the transmission of ideas, pointing to Sulpicius Severus and John Cassian, who, although western, owe many of their ideas to eastern desert culture.

21. Frank (1998, 488) uses the example of Theodoret's *Religious History* to argue that the genre of travel writing was dropped, as if this were a conscious decision. This is repeated in her book (2000, 41). She even argues that miracles are a feature of travel writing, as if this is why we find them in the *History of the Monks of Egypt!* (1998, 490; 2000, 44–45). Cf. her own citation of Bowersock (1994, 14) in Frank 2000, 38.

22. See my later discussion.

23. Miller 2000, 221.

monks of Syria, and thus drawing attention to their similarity by simply putting them in the collection, but also drawing distinctions between them.

Both authors call their work a *historia,* both claim to be eyewitnesses and say that their opera will be useful for themselves as well as their readers, both warn that their tales may sound incredible but of course are true, and both say that it is impossible to do their subjects justice. In both cases, all this information is contained in the prologues. These similarities support the argument that Theodoret was aiming to create a work that would show that Syria had spiritual heroes equivalent to those of Egypt.[24] He does not speculate as to why this might be, but the author of the *History of the Monks of Egypt* pondered the special nature of Egypt and concluded that it was a land of extremes. In the past, Egyptians had been extremely sinful, worshiping dogs, monkeys, and even vegetables. Now Egypt was an extremely holy place.

So there are very similar sentiments in the prologues of both works about the task in hand and its purpose. In the body of the *History of the Monks of Egypt* one can find the same features about holy men that are included in the *Religious History.* Monks eat very little, wear irons and chains, stand all night, sleep very little, do not allow women to come near them, and communicate only through windows. One might object that there are only a limited number of ways in which individuals can test their physical endurance.[25] But there are other shared items: the monks are helped by angels, perform miracles and healings, and utter prophecies. Generally they withdraw from the world, but they also form communities.[26] In both works, there is mention of the native language of the area to show that all levels of the population can be reached. The *Religious History* mentions only Greek and Syriac, while the biographies in the *History of the Monks of Egypt* usually include Latin as well as Greek

---

24. See, for instance, Canivet 1977, 77. Fowden (1999, 92–93) argues that monks used group biographies to propagate the communal way of life, citing the *History of the Monks of Egypt* and the *Lausiac History* as works that did much to crystallize the ascetic way of life. While this may have been true for the Egyptian works, it is not clear that the same can be argued for Theodoret's work, given its literary style and later composition, since the asceticism seems to have been well established by the time he wrote.

25. See Vööbus 1960, 298–300, on the originality of the Syrians.

26. Judge (1977, 77–78) notes that the term *monachos* appears for the first time in the *Life of Antony* precisely when Antony abandons his solitude.

and Coptic.[27] The issue of language is raised in the *History of the Monks of Egypt* to emphasize knowledge, not ignorance: Theon knew Latin, Greek, and Coptic (6). In both works, there are references to contemporary political events.

However there are details that Theodoret did not borrow or adapt in any way: the author of the *History of the Monks of Egypt* informs us that he is not a cleric (1) and explains the circumstances of the work. He says he traveled, at some danger to his person, from Jerusalem to Egypt (Prologue 14, 18–19) in order to gather information about the monks there. In the epilogue he provides a list of all the dangers he encountered. He opens a large number of the chapters with expressions such as "we saw," thus immediately insisting that this is an eyewitness account. Theodoret's tale is not recounted by a fascinated visitor but that of a knowledgeable insider who can claim long-standing personal friendships with a number of his subjects. A striking difference between the two works is that in the *History of the Monks of Egypt* some monks tell of other monks, that is, we get stories within stories, so that the whole account is not directly from the author but a relation of what others have told him. The most obvious example is the tale in which the monk Copres, although asked to describe his way of life, tells the author about the lives of others "better than he" (chapters 10–12).

In the Egyptian work there is more emphasis on the astonishingly huge numbers of monks living in the places to which the author traveled. For instance, he tells us that Oxyrhynchus was full of monasteries (chapter 5). The bishop had ten thousand monks and twenty thousand virgins under him. Another noticeable feature is that there is much more sexual temptation. In contrast there is very little at all in the *Religious History.* There is the curious tale about Eusebius and his plowmen, but the sexual element may be in the perversity of the modern eye. Eusebius had been taking rather more interest in the plowmen working in the nearby field than in listening to the theological discussion led by Ammianus. After being rebuked for this he never looked at them again for forty years, and to help in his resolve he wore an iron belt and very heavy collar, which forced him to bend down toward the ground (*Religious History* 4.6). For sexual tempta-

---

27. See Bagnall 1993, 235–40, on Coptic, and 244–45 on the languages of Egyptian monks.

tion, one should always try Jerome first, whose life of Paul of Thebes is astonishing even for him.[28]

The *History of the Monks of Egypt* is also much racier than the *Religious History,* containing as it does stories of monks being seduced (1.32–35), monks being accused of fornication (16), discussions of how to prevent ejaculation (20), and men catching their wives committing adultery (24).[29] It also gives a more vivid picture of the material setting since it features animals as well as ascetics, for example, a hippopotamus (4), a snake (9), a crocodile (12), and a hyena (21). Jerome, on the other hand, likes lions.[30] Two of them dig Paul's grave to help out the elderly Antony, who is stuck with the saint's corpse but has no spade (*Life of Paul of Thebes* 15), and a lion kills Malchus's master and slave when they try to take him back into slavery (*Life of Malchus* 6). Another aspect lacking in Theodoret's work is the large numbers of robbers and bandits who become monks (e.g., *History of the Monks of Egypt* 6, 10). One might argue that this feature does not reflect well on the monasteries, as it could be interpreted as saying that they were full of criminals. Perhaps this is the reason for there being none in Theodoret's work.

It has been suggested that Theodoret was deliberately writing a counterpart to Palladius's *Lausiac History,* a work written in 419–20 that was well known by the first half of the fifth century. However there are not as many similarities as one might expect if this were the case.[31] There are, for one thing, many more lives in Palladius' account

---

28. Jerome opens this life with a little historical background and then relates the torments that troubled the martyrs of the time: "A beautiful prostitute came up to him and began to stroke his neck with gentle caresses and (what is improper even to relate) to touch his private parts with her hands: when his body was roused to lust as a result, this shameful conqueress lay down on top of him. The soldier of Christ did not know what to do or where to turn: he who had not yielded to tortures was being overcome by pleasure. At last, by divine inspiration, he bit off his tongue and spat it in her face as she kissed him; and so the sense of lust was overcome by sharp pain that replaced it" (*Life of Paul of Thebes* 3). Jerome's *Life of Malchus* is also a story of chastity. Benedict solved the problem in a similar way. When disturbed by lust he threw himself into nettles and brambles according to Gregory the Great (*Life of Benedict* 2.1–2).

29. The *Lausiac History* has a similar fascination with sex: there are attempted seductions of slave girls (3), women who shut themselves away in tombs because men find them attractive (5), virgins who live in sin (28), and monks who lust after virgins (29).

30. See Elliott 1987, 144–67, on animals in saints' lives.

31. Dagron 1970, 259, n. 152. On the *Lausiac History,* see Turner 1905. See Hunt 1973, 458–60, on the similarities between the *Lausiac History* and the *History of the Monks of Egypt.* For an overview of this literature, see Hofmann 1997, 447–50.

and it is directed to a specific person, Lausus. That said, the main aspect they have in common is the continuous presence of the author as a participant, in both cases a bishop who was a former monk and the friend of his subjects.[32] The author of the *History of the Monks of Egypt* was also present but as an outsider, a visitor from Jerusalem, whereas Palladius claimed to have lived among these monks and known some of them personally, this being the reason why he wrote in the first place. Unlike Theodoret, he does not appear in his role as bishop in this work. His anecdotes are very lively, feature more animals (although not as many as are found in the *History of the Monks of Egypt*), and include many more women than does the *Religious History.* Melania plays what could be seen as a similar role to that of Theodoret's mother since she is a source for some of the stories (e.g., 5 and 9), although she is more awesome, having achieved an elevated status herself.[33]

An aspect Theodoret did not imitate in his work is the rather entertaining notion of the lapsed monk (e.g., *Lausiac History* 25, 26, 27, 28). Palladius explains that he thinks it good to include a record of those who failed as a warning not to become smug (25). He even records his own failure as a monk, although this was due to illness rather than a moral inadequacy (2).[34] He also includes demons and horribly grotesque stories, with physical illness or deformity described in unwelcome detail (see, e.g., 11, 12, 15, and especially 17, which includes a young man so sick that he eats his own excrement, and 18, wherein we read of a holy man who punishes himself for killing a gnat by sitting in a marsh for six months and becoming so swollen with bites that when he returns he is only recognizable by his voice, about someone with cancer of the head so far gone that the bone shows through, and about a possessed boy who swells up and emits liquid from all his sense organs). The work is more immediate and lively, containing more sex and gore and written in easier Greek than Theodoret's version, leading to the suggestion that the imagined audience was not the same and the *Lausiac History* was aimed at a less educated class of people. Monks are not portrayed as subser-

---

32. See Buck 1976 on Palladius writing the *Lausiac History* and basing the structure on his own life.

33. See Moine 1980; Hunt 1973, 463–64, 477–80; and Murphy 1947 on Melania.

34. Jerome comments that one's mind tends to wander during prayer, which Theodoret would never have admitted (*Life of Hilarion* 8).

vient to bishops, and we get no sense of a distinction between the established church and the ascetics, something that does emerge in the *Religious History*.

Theodoret's work follows a tradition of Christian biography. It belongs to a recognizable type, that is, the collection of lives of holy men from a particular area. But it is not simply an exercise in hagiography. There are too many apparently puzzling features for that. The author is in too central a position. It is from a comparison with works of a similar sort that Theodoret's originality emerges clearly.[35] It is written in a higher literary style and the monks are presented in a uniformly hagiographic way, with no failures or unseemly obsessions with sex among them.[36] They perform miracles and are all from northern Syria. There is certainly variety among them but not as much as in other works given the constraints mentioned earlier. Crucially, the one individual who eclipses them all, in a way other authors do not, is Theodoret.

Before going on to look specifically at Theodoret's presence in the work and how he is portrayed, it is necessary to examine what he claims he is setting out to do and what he concludes he has done by taking a closer look at his prologue and epilogue.

---

35. There are no self-reflexive moments in the *Religious History* such as we see in the *Life of Daniel,* where we learn Daniel would not allow a life of himself to be written or a portrait painted (12). Cf. Theodore of Sykeon, who blessed a picture of himself (*Life of Theodore of Sykeon* 139). For a further but later parallel, see the *Vita Patrum,* which is discussed by Elliott (1987, 11–12), includes lives of Antony and Symeon Stylites as well as Ephraim, and used Theodoret's *Religious History* and Palladius' *Lausiac History* (13).

36. See Patlagean (1983, 103) on the problems of determining the intended audience for saints' lives.

Chapter 4

The Aims of the *Religious History:* The Prologue and Epilogue

Theodoret makes a number of important claims for his work at both the start and the finish. It may be that his programmatic statements are mere formulas, but I wish to look at what he explicitly sets out to do, even if he does not carry out these intentions. The prologue to the *Religious History* has been described as "an elegant tissue of commonplaces," but it is different from those of similar works, even though one can find echoing sentiments.[1] It would be very easy to dismiss the prefaces of many modern scholarly works as being clumsy patchworks of clichés, but most readers would admit that they do say something significant about how the text was intended to be viewed. I will also discuss the treatise called *On Divine Love,* which purports to be an epilogue to the work and is found following the main text of *Religious History* in some manuscripts.

The prologue is a very formal opening to the work and is a place where one might expect to find a programmatic statement or generalization about the nature of the work to follow. It consists of eleven paragraphs in which Theodoret explains why he is writing. The structure of his argument is as follows: it is good to record the feats of admirable people in writing since otherwise we would forget them; we remember other sorts of heroes like actors and athletes; the

---

1. Price 1985a, 10; see also Canivet 1977, 65–66. See Festugière 1960, 129–37, on topoi in prologues in hagiographical works. The *Religious History* was not written at the behest of anyone, unlike the *Lausiac History.* Theodoret may be showing that he is writing on his own initiative (Leppin 1996a, 229). The prologue to the *Lausiac History,* in which Palladius presents his work to Lausus, is genuine, but the proemium that precedes it is not, says Draguet (1946).

Christians are warriors of a sort and these ascetics fight evil, defeating it by means of their ascetic practices (and therefore they should be recorded); Theodoret will provide a selection of these lives; and readers should believe what they read since it is the truth and Theodoret was an eyewitness in many cases.

Some of these sentiments can be found in the prologues to the other works mentioned, but none corresponds exactly and it is productive to see what Theodoret chooses to tell his readers. His first observation is that the work will benefit both those who read it and himself. The idea that history is useful was a standard one since it provided models to copy or examples to avoid for future generations. The expression of this idea most familiar to ancient historians is found in Thucydides 1.22.4.[2] Biography has a similar didactic purpose since it sets out to show the qualities necessary to make great statesmen.[3] The authors of the lives of holy men and women took this idea a step further and commented that they would be helped by simply telling the story.[4] It is an idea that occurs in the prologues to the *Life of Antony* and the *History of the Monks of Egypt*.

Theodoret draws attention to the fact that one might be inclined to believe what one sees rather than what one hears, but he says that we believe our ears when we judge the speaker to be truthful. This is all in the first paragraph. Immediately, then, he introduces the issue of credibility, reinforcing his own account and perhaps implicitly drawing attention to the deficiencies of others. Asserting the veracity of one's account and explaining one's method of working to build trust

---

2. "It will be enough for me, however, if these words of mine are judged useful by those who want to understand clearly the events which happened in the past and which [human nature being what it is] will at some time or other and in much the same ways, be repeated in the future. My work is not a piece of writing designed to meet the taste of an immediate public but was done to last for ever." Translated by Rex Warner for Penguin in *Thucydides: The Peloponnesian War* (Harmondsworth, 1954), 48.

3. Wardman has observed this (1971, 256). Cox (1983, 5) insists that biography was not a subgenre of history and that truth was not one of its characteristics. Woodman (1988, 197), of course, would say that it was not one of history's either. However, while agreeing that biography was not a subgenre of history I would think it hardly likely that any biographer would admit to writing anything but the truth. Tabloids are well known for their economy with the truth, but their power lies precisely in people's belief in their claim to be providing it. For a refreshing antidote to all such protestations of truth telling, see Lucian's prologue to his *True History*.

4. See Xenophon's comment that Socrates was useful even for those who were remembering him is a precursor of this (*Memorabilia* 4.1.1). Sulpicius Severus ends his life of Martin of Tours with a carefully worded wish: "And the reward prepared by God, as I hope, will await not whoever reads this but whoever believes it"!

in the reader is very common in history writing. In the case of a monument to Syrian ascetics, such a reassurance is perhaps necessary, especially if Theodoret was writing for the intellectual elite of Constantinople or at least Antioch and Alexandria.[5]

In the next two paragraphs, he provides an elaborate justification for his narrative, arguing that it is right to preserve the memory of these holy individuals, especially considering that less worthy people have been commemorated. Theodoret compares his task to that of poets, historians, tragedians, and comic writers. In different literary forms they all celebrate human achievement, which is also what Theodoret wishes to do.[6] How much one should read into it is debatable, but it is certainly useful to be alert to the fact that Theodoret is strongly emphasizing his classical connections. He does not seem to be making any distinction between the status of narratives in poetry and history, but rather groups poets with historians, saying that they record acts of bravery in war. The difference is one of form, poetry, and prose, not subject matter.

He is also placing his work in the line of classical compositions, although his is superior because of the nature of its subject. This must reflect the makeup of Theodoret's intended readership — that is, they are classically educated. The first sentence of the work uses a typically classical metaphor, calling the ascetics athletes, and that imagery is used throughout.[7] Theodoret was not innovating here. Classical allusions permeate the works of Jerome, who, for example, refers explicitly to Sallust in his prologue to the *Life of Hilarion* and, a little unexpectedly, includes a centaur and a satyr in his *Life of Paul of Thebes* (chapters 7–8).[8] After describing the centaur he comments that this was either the work of the devil or one of the monstrous creatures produced by the desert. In the episode in which the satyr appears the creature is described with no such proviso, perhaps because this monster was a Christian. Indeed, he claims that when it died the corpse was sprinkled with salt to preserve it and then taken to Antioch to show to the emperor. Sulpicius Severus also begins his *Life of Martin* with a glance back to classical

---

5. Quasten (1960, 528) calls Theodoret's Greek "perfect, and his style clear and simple."

6. Canivet makes rather a lot of this (1977, 66–70).

7. See Spadavecchia 1985 on the use of this metaphor in Theodoret's work.

8. See Fuhrmann 1976 on Jerome's preface to his *Life of Hilarion.*

works, if only to discard them, commenting that no one ever benefitted from reading about Hector or Socrates. The Egyptian works, on the other hand, parade no such learning, suggesting a less sophisticated readership.

Theodoret expostulates that if athletes, charioteers, and men who look like women, by which he presumably means actors, are all recorded for posterity in some way then surely holy men should be.[9] Here he is using athletes as examples of individuals less worthy of commemoration than holy men, and yet he uses the metaphor of the athletic contest continually. One implication of this metaphor is that the ascetics were competing with each other for prizes. One wonders how admirable this is. Generally, he acknowledges that ordinary athletes are worthy of the honor of a memorial but thinks ascetics are even more so. His addition of effeminate men, or perhaps transvestites, is a little jarring, but his comment presumably reflects the frequency with which actors had their portraits painted.[10] He continues by explaining that the *Religious History* is not a painting but a sketch in words of the souls of the ascetics and their unseen wars and secret struggles.

Introducing his next line of argument with quotations from Paul, he declares that the *Religious History* will describe wars. This might strike readers as a little odd or unexpected, especially once they have read it, but it should be remembered that it was called a history, which many might argue is a series of wars.[11] He says that it will recount the victory of individuals over their bodies and demons. It does not in fact do this, and Theodoret concentrates much less on this aspect than do the accounts of the Egyptian monks. None of these works, although they are indeed about this kind of struggle, declare this in their prologues.

9. There are verses describing pictures of courtesans in *The Greek Anthology* (translated in Paton 1916–1918), for instance, 16:77, 78, 80. I am grateful to Alan Cameron for drawing my attention to these poems. See Cameron 1993 on this collection generally. See Bowersock 2000, 257–59 on the Syriac *Life of Rabbula* and the use of the imagery of painting to describe biography.

10. The prologue (3) says that all these types of people have their portraits painted on panels. In the prologue to the *Ecclesiastical History* he also compares painters and historians, saying that painters paint on panels and walls whereas historians substitute books for panels and that words last longer than pictures.

11. See, for instance, Eusebius's comments in his preface to book 5 of his *Ecclesiastical History*. See also Socrates, *Ecclesiastical History* 5, preface, discussed by Urbainczyk 1997a, 69–70.

At the end of his struggle, the holy man's perceptions change and become utterly different from those of ordinary people. This is an opportunity for Theodoret to present a very clever series of paradoxes, but it also represents the holy man as exotic.[12] He considers fasting to be feasting, arduous work to be pleasant rest, the hard ground to be a soft bed, and a life of prayer to be a pleasure (7). Their practices are very strange to the classically educated Greek aristocrat and if the reader feels a certain repulsion, this may have been at least partly Theodoret's intention. He builds them up as different from ordinary people which automatically renders them objects of fear.[13] His work would be far less effective if they were merely seen as deeply pious. These mavericks did pose a significant threat to the established church when they were not under the authority of a bishop. They were individuals who rejected society and thus, implicitly, the church. They could easily have formed a new community of Christians parallel to, and antagonistic to, those living and flourishing in the cities. It may be that such unease on the part of clerics is reflected in Theodoret's work, or alternatively it may have served his purpose to portray them as a potential threat.

He then says that he will not write a single eulogy (εὐφημία) because the individuals are all different; rather, he will describe each one and his or her peculiarities. This is interesting because he is admitting that he is writing eulogy or praise. In eulogy, of course, it was customary to deny that one was writing eulogy. However, Theodoret is not making this point directly; he is explaining how he is going about his task. He will not write some composite work but a series, focusing on one individual after another, which is what he does. It will hardly come as a surprise to the reader to learn that he or she will read praise since that is the justification for writing in the first place and these are models of virtue. His point is not that this is truth rather than panegyric, which is what is at stake when panegyrists deny their genre, but rather that this will be a series of lives rather than one long account. Also he is saying that there will be variety, since this is why he cannot write one long account. In other words, the reader can expect to be entertained. Later, in the course of the work, he has a

---

12. Goehring (1992) argues that Theodoret's Hellenistic filter distorts the picture of Syrian monasticism. See also Vööbus on this kind of asceticism (1960, 256–78).

13. At 27.1, he lists all the varieties of asceticism he has described in the *Religious History*. This passage is discussed in chapter 6.

whole paragraph on the variety of holy men he has described (*Religious History* 27.1).[14]

He also reassures his readers that there will be only a few details, a selection, from the lives of the ascetics, through which each character is revealed. This will remind the well read of Plutarch's comments at the start of his life of Alexander, where he says that he will use minor events, sayings, and jests to reveal character. Wardman points out that Plutarch raises the issue in that particular place because there was so much material on Alexander.[15] He also argues that the three aspects Plutarch mentions, that is, minor events, sayings, and jests, are derived from history, which could be said to deal with great events, both military and political, interspersed with speeches. Biography is thus history on a small scale. One can apply this to Theodoret's *Religious History* and *Ecclesiastical History:* hagiography can be seen as an offshoot of church history, since it deals with the individuals who are characters making up the larger picture, and some of Theodoret's holy men also feature in his church history. Hagiography, like Plutarch's biographies, focuses on the qualities necessary for success.

Theodoret adds that he cannot mention all the ascetics since there are too many; he will record only the stars. By "stars" he seems to mean the most famous ones because he says "So I shall record the life of those alone who have appeared like stars in the east and reached the end of the world with their rays" (Prologue 9). Again this promises the reader only the best while perhaps recalling the claim made by Palladius, at the opening of his work, that he would describe all the individuals in cities, villages, and the desert (*Lausiac History,* Prologue 16). Theodoret's statement conveniently assures readers that there are too many ascetics in Syria to record them all, so it does not matter if he does not include as many as are found in other works. Toward the end of paragraph 9, he says that he will proceed in narrative form and not follow the rules of panegyric. Menander Rhetor describes these in his *basilikos logos,* wherein he tells us that in a panegyric one should give details of the individual's family, country, early life, and deeds according to virtue.[16] It is true that

---

14. See chapter 6.

15. Wardman 1971. See also Duff 1999, 14–22.

16. See Russell and Wilson 1981, 76–95, for the Menander Rhetor text of the *basilikos logos.* See also the discussion in Russell 1998.

generally Theodoret does not discuss these aspects. When at the end of the life of Jacob of Cyrrhestica (*Religious History* 21.35) he says that he wrote this in the form of a narrative not a panegyric, his words should be taken literally. The form is not panegyric, but the content is.[17] He finishes paragraph 9 of the prologue by saying that his narration will be written ἀτεχνῶς. This can mean "simply" or "sincerely," but in this context it must mean "without art" because he has just said that he will not be following the rules of panegyric. This in itself is a topos and most palpably untrue in Theodoret's case.[18]

Having described his purpose and method, he explains that his work should be believed because he was an eyewitness or had heard from eyewitnesses (Prologue 11). In a disarming comparison between his work and the Gospels, he argues that Luke and Mark are given as much credibility as Matthew and John, although they were not eyewitnesses.[19] He does, however, subscribe to the conventional view that an eyewitness account is superior to all others since he is asking to be believed precisely because he was an eyewitness. Understandably, this emphasis on the status of the testimony is a feature found in the *Life of Antony,* the *History of the Monks of Egypt,* and the *Lausiac History.*[20] The authors of these works all stress that they have personally seen what they are about to relate or that they have heard from those who have. Jerome, on the other hand, although he is able to tell us (for instance) that Hilarion had visions of naked women (7), and from the age of thirty-one to thirty-five ate only six ounces of barley bread and lightly cooked vegetables without any oil (presumably daily, 11), does not disclose his sources.

Theodoret, in a passage reminiscent of Thucydides, asks his readers not to measure the holy men against themselves and thus disbelieve the miracles about which they read.[21] He acknowledges that the

---

17. See Canivet 1977, 65–82, on the literary genre, especially 70–71 on panegyric.

18. Οὐ νόμοις ἐγκωμίων χρώμενος, ἀλλ᾽ ὀλίγων τινῶν ἀτεχνῶς ποιούμενος τὴν διήγησιν.

19. See Canivet and Molinghen 1977, 158–59, on the hierarchy of the evangelists. See Krueger 1997b on Theodoret's comparisons with biblical precedents.

20. Lane Fox (1997, 203–4) discusses hagiographers on their sources, pointing out that they, unlike historians, do not criticize or distance themselves from them but rather arrange their narratives so that the reader believes and marvels.

21. Pericles in his funeral speech comments that those who know the dead will think he is not praising them enough while those who do not will not believe it out of jealousy since most people cannot bear to hear praise about exploits they could not have achieved themselves (Thucydides, *History* 2.35).

reader will meet events that stretch their credulity but, in another comparison which elevates his own work rather strikingly, he had challenged the reader in the previous paragraph (10), saying that if they believed the Bible they ought to believe this. There are apparently incredible stories in the Bible that, as a good Christian, one should believe. If one is a good Christian and believes them, then one will believe Theodoret.[22] This multipurpose condition raises the status of his writing to an apostolic level, silences the questioning reader and promises a tale of epic proportions. He ends saying he has protested the truth of his account for too long and will now start the narrative. The prologue is, above all else, an effective advertisement for the work as a whole, promising an entertaining, varied, perhaps amazing tale, which will also be good for its readers.

On Divine Love

The *Religious History* ends in a rather puzzling way. Theodoret appears to make concluding remarks at the end of the life of Domnina, but in many manuscripts there is also a treatise called *On Divine Love,* which at least presents itself as generalizing remarks about the preceding lives of holy men. The life of Domnina is extremely brief, and only three of the eight paragraphs deal with the subject. The rest say that there are many women like her and many monasteries of men and women throughout the east. He lists Palestine, Egypt, Asia, Pontus, Europe, Syria, Cilicia, and Mesopotamia (*Religious History* 30.5–6). He explains that he has added accounts of female ascetics so that women will have models to follow, and he presents an extended analogy about painters having models and joiners using a rule to measure expressing the hope that his readers and those about whom he has written will pray for him. Given that the idea of the painter takes us back to the prologue (3), one might assume that this is Theodoret's conclusion.[23]

---

22. Jerome had a similarly challenging approach to his readers. In his *Life of Paul of Thebes* he says, after describing the dietary habits of his hero, "These things will appear incredible only to those who do not believe that everything is possible for those who believe" (6). This echoes Mark 9.22–23: "But Jesus said to him, 'If thou canst believe, to him who believes, everything is possible.'"

23. See also the prologue to his *Ecclesiastical History,* where he uses this analogy.

However, in both Canivet and Leroy-Molinghen's edition and Price's English translation there is a treatise called *On Divine Love*. As the treatise does not appear in all the manuscripts, it has sometimes been ignored and sometimes rejected as inauthentic. Canivet and Leroy-Molinghen justify their inclusion of it by pointing out that most of the oldest manuscripts have *On Divine Love* included with the *Religious History* and that from an analysis of its style and content they think it was written by Theodoret.[24] It seems undeniable that the short piece was intended to follow the *Religious History* since it refers to the writing of lives in its opening lines. Whether it was written by Theodoret would seem to be very difficult to determine. Canivet points out the many echoes between this and other works by Theodoret, while allowing that the ancients possessed great skill in imitating style.[25] Price accepts its authenticity, adding that he does not think it was part of the original edition of the *Religious History,* but he observes that it is impossible to date.[26]

One might wish to suggest that the original work ended with the life of Symeon Stylites (26), given the nature of the very brief subsequent lives, which are not in the same order in all the manuscripts.[27] Canivet and Leroy-Molinghen also argue that the long introduction to the life of Baradatus (27) is oddly placed, being more suited either to the first of those from Cyrrhestica or to the account of Symeon himself.[28] Given these oddities, the addition of a treatise by Theodoret himself is not out of the question, and as it has often been treated as part of the whole work it is worth considering here. It seems entirely possible that Theodoret did revise the *Religious History,* adding the last four lives and the treatise *On Divine Love*. The title of this piece differs from manuscript to manuscript (περὶ ἀγάπης, περὶ θείας ἀγάπης, and περὶ τῆς θείας ἀγάπης) and there is no mention of the author's name except in one case.[29] So what exactly does the treatise say?

The author begins by referring to the main work: "How great and how many are the athletes of virtue and with which crowns they are

24. Canivet 1966.

25. Ibid. See also Price 1985a, 207.

26. Price (ibid., 206) thinks that it was part of an otherwise unchanged second edition, but it would be odd to produce a second edition merely to add this treatise.

27. Devos 1979, 335; Canivet 1977, 84.

28. Canivet and Leroy-Molinghen 1977–79, 219, n. 4.

29. Canivet 1966, 147.

decked, is clearly demonstrated by the accounts we have written of them" (*On Divine Love* 1).[30] He goes on to say that he has not included all their feats of endurance since a few are enough to give a sense of their character, picking up the point he made in the prologue (8) that he will not be narrating every fact about each individual's life. He goes on to say that one tests coins by rubbing a little of them against a stone and then uses the analogy of a skill. Just as one can perceive a skill from a few actions, so one can perceive virtue similarly, a very classical analogy, which one might expect from Theodoret.[31] So he begins by admitting that he has not recorded everything but explains that one can infer a way of life from a few instances. He goes on to say that the purpose of the work at hand is to discover the reasons why these individuals lived the way they did, that is, how it was they achieved their virtue.

He admits that others endure physical hardship but explains the reasons why the holy men were different. He compares them first to shepherds and points out that, although these men may have to live in the open, they eat as much food as they want, which keeps the body warmer than any clothing. Similarly, other workers such as sailors, farm laborers and shepherds may suffer adversity but they rest and take measures to ease their discomfort; moreover, they have wives at home. The ascetics have none of these, and therefore their achievements are far greater. The author's first wish, then, is to dispense with the idea that other people undergo similar privations. The ascetics are different, and no one is their equal in their fortitude. Having established this, he explains that it is a desire for God that propels them. The language he uses is very sensuous, and the influence of the *Song of Songs* is very strong in the treatise. It is mentioned explicitly twice (*On Divine Love* 5, 19). The longing and yearning for God is the motivation for the holy man, and, although physical desire can be satisfied, there is no fill of divine desire, the author remarks.

This, of course, is what the treatise is showing—that these individuals do odd things through love of God. The author goes on to say that Moses felt this fervor, too, and this was what drove him (*On*

---

30. Translations of the *Religious History* are those of Price, except where noted otherwise.
31. See, for example, Plato's *Republic* (1.342a–e). See also Plutarch, *Life of Alexander* 1.

Divine Love 5). Paul also has things to say about love, and the treatise is filled with biblical references, far more so than in the *Religious History*. If we love God we do not care about hardships, and after an extended discussion of this he moves on to the relationship between Peter and Christ.[32] Christ asked Peter repeatedly whether he loved him, and Peter, remembering his previous denial, lost confidence in his assertions and admitted that Christ knows the truth and the future better than he. Christ welcomes his humility and reassures Peter.

We then read about the latter's crucifixion. This takes up a large proportion of the text, and its relevance is not immediately obvious except that we see an expression of love for Christ and the ultimate sacrifice. The author goes on to say that the goods of the world are ephemeral whereas only virtue lasts. And virtue really is love of God. Then there is a series of Old Testament figures who also showed a great love of God, except Adam, who starts off the series as the counterexample. The centerpiece is Abraham, who is rather godlike in that he is willing to let his son die (*On Divine Love* 17). Eventually the author says that he will not go on with this list. Now that he has shown how the prophets achieved virtue he returns to the new athletes.[33]

> It was enamored of this beauty that the new athletes of virtue also, whose life we have recorded in brief, have leapt into those great conflicts that surpass human nature. This they were taught clearly by the divine Scriptures. (19)

If this treatise performs any function then one could say it is refuting two criticisms: (1) that other people endure similar hardships and (2) that these ascetics are too odd. Theodoret, if it is he who wrote it, replies that other people do not perform the same feats and that his heroes have precedents in the Bible. They are showing a zeal that one can read about in the Old and New Testaments. Again the language is reminiscent of the *Song of Songs,* with great longing for the beauty of the bridegroom.

The final paragraph is the most curious. There the author says that

---

32. Canivet (1977, 99–101) shows the similarities between this passage and part of Theodore of Mopsuestia's Commentary on John the Apostle.

33. The use of the athletic image is frequent in the *Religious History.*

the holy men are like the biblical figures mentioned and that we, too, ought to love God in a similarly intense way:

> Let us become bewitched by the beauty of the Bridegroom, eager for the promised goods, paying heed to the multitude of benefits, fearing the punishment for ingratitude, and so in our love be maintainers of his laws. (*On Divine Love* 21)

And suddenly a different tone emerges. This, says the author, is the definition of *friendship* (φιλία), that is, to like and hate the same things, in essence to have the same friends and enemies.[34] The introduction of hatred is rather jarring, even though one might argue that the treatise is about love and hate is the opposite of love. But it is not introduced in this way, and the result is strange. Then there is another swift and unexpected transition: there are quotations from the psalms about hating the enemies of one's friends, and then we move on to hating the lawbreakers and loving the law. The next step, that love (ἀγάπη) is obedience, is the most disturbing. The author says: "The clear proof of love for God is the keeping of his divine laws. 'He who loves me will keep my commandments,' says Christ the Master" (21). This is discordant with the tone of the rest of the piece, wherein the ideas of hatred, enemies, enforcement, and restrictions are completely absent. The shift is puzzling, although perhaps not for the cynical reader who might wish to see this as the work of a bishop trying to keep some order among unruly parishioners or wishing to strengthen the message of some of the canons of the Council of Chalcedon, which reinforced the obedience of monks to bishops. The tone of the work is very different from that of the *Religious History,* and one can see why scholars have doubted its authenticity and its place.

In the prologue Theodoret represents his work as an act of piety and celebration. He is rescuing these ascetics from oblivion and providing models for his readers to follow and thus be saved and achieve the greatest good. The models he holds up will be varied and almost

---

34. Plato (*Republic* 1.334b) uses a similar definition for justice — it is helping friends and harming enemies. See Konstan 1997, 58, on these implications of friendship. Cf. Thucydides 1.36, where the Corcyrans claim they are the friends of the Athenians because they have a common enemy in the Corinthians; and 1.41, where the Corinthians respond that they have helped Athens in the past and thus deserve some loyalty.

incredible, but the faithful should believe them. The epilogue, *On Divine Love,* defends his work from potential or actual critics, claiming that his heroes are more admirable than workers since they never eat their fill and have no wives to look after them. His heroes are odd, but they are holy, and they do what they do out of love for God, hence the title of the piece. A rather later date for its composition could account for its change in tone, but nevertheless it makes surprising reading at the end of the *Religious History.* It is far less direct and entertaining, despite having many more sensuous images. It has many more biblical quotations, which break up its flow, and it ends on a most disconcerting note, saying that love is obedience to orders.[35]

35. It is of course true that Theodoret means one should obey divine orders, but see Gould 1993, 53, on obedience being a very special virtue for monks. Rousseau (1978, 165) describes the values Sulpicius Severus extols for churchmen in his life of Martin of Tours. See MacDermot 1971, 29–30, on the growing emphasis on obedience for monks.

PART II

The Heroes of the *Religious History*

Chapter 5

Who Were the Holy Men?
Their Background and Role

In this chapter I wish to look at the heroes of Theodoret's work. What kind of individuals are they? Are they as he has described them in his prologue and epilogue or has he misrepresented them? It is also useful to consider them against the notion of the collection, that is, to see how similar they are to each other, looking at their background, what language they spoke, and what they did.[1]

On another occasion, when the city was driven insane by some evil demon and vented its frenzy against the imperial statues,[2] the supreme generals arrived with a verdict of total destruction against the city. He [Macedonius] descended from the mountain and stopped the two generals as they were crossing the square; on learning who it was, they leapt down from their horses, clasped his hands and knees and asked for his salutation. He charged them to tell the emperor that he was a man, with the same nature as those who had acted outrageously, that while anger ought to be proportionate to one's nature, he had given rein to anger that was out of proportion: because of his own images he was consigning to execution the images of God and for the sake of bronze statues delivering bodies to death. "It is easy and simply for us" he continued, "to remold and refashion bronze figures, but it is impossible for you, even though you are emperor, to bring back to life bodies you have slaughtered. And why do I say bodies? You cannot refashion

---
1. See Cox Miller 2000 on the notion of the collection.
2. For a narrative of this episode, see Downey 1961, 426–33.

a single hair." He said this in Syriac; and while the interpreter translated it into Greek, the generals shuddered as they listened, and promised to convey this message to the emperor. (*Religious History* 13.7)

In this passage, Theodoret portrays the ideal holy man. He comes to help when communities are in trouble, in this case due to a demon; he has far-reaching influence, since the generals know and respect him. He rebukes the emperor, the ultimate human authority but one who holds no threats for a monk. He speaks in the language of the common man, and his words have to be translated so that members of the ruling class can understand. When they do, they shudder. What we have here is Browning's "counter-hero of the dispossessed and of those to whom the high urban culture of Late Antiquity had nothing to offer."[3] Even more romantically expressed, Drijvers translates this as "The holy man broke through all social boundaries and classes and represented help and justice in the merciless social structure of an ancient city, in which a stranger especially was a social outcast."[4] Yet Theodoret's passage quoted out of context gives a rather misleading impression of the way in which he depicts holy men.

Theodoret's work performs three functions. First, it argues for a prominent position for Syria in ecclesiastical affairs by demonstrating that it, as well as Egypt, has produced individuals remarkable for their piety. Second, it portrays these as deferring to the church, thus providing a model for how ascetics should behave. Third, it demonstrates the unique authority Theodoret enjoys in this region. In the following chapters I wish to demonstrate how effectively he achieves these points.

First, I consider the people whom he chose to portray, what their social background was, what language they spoke, and how they lived. A typical description reads: "Monks came from different social and cultural backgrounds, but in many regions of the eastern Roman empire, they were mostly peasants."[5] This is a common view, as Canivet points out.

---

3. Browning 1981, 127.
4. Drijvers 1981, 28.
5. Bowersock, Brown, and Grabar 1999, 586.

Les modernes soulignent à leur tour l'absence de culture intellectuelle chez les moines d'Orient, en s'appuyant sur le témoignage des hagiographes qui montrent la superiorité de la sainteté sur la culture.[6]

The poverty of the holy man is often emphasized in our texts, and yet it is surprisingly uncommon to find one who started off poor.[7] More frequently these holy individuals were from the upper echelons of society.[8] Antony's family was well born we are told (*Life of Antony*). So were, for example, Hilarion, Paul, Malchus, Martin of Tours, Melania, John the Almsgiver, and Benedict.[9] Theodore of Sykeon was the son of a prostitute and a circus acrobat, but his case is less common than one might assume (*Life of Theodore* 3).[10]

If we learn anything at all about the social origins of Theodoret's heroes it is most often that they are from noble families. He specifies only three instances in the whole work in which his subjects are from poor backgrounds. There are Macedonius, who spoke Syriac and had a rustic upbringing (*Religious History* 13.7–8), and Maësymas, whom he describes in a very similar way, that is, "who was Syrian in his language and had had a rustic upbringing," Σύρος μὲν τὴν φωνήν, ἐν ἀγροικίᾳ δὲ τεθραμμένος (14.2). It should be noted that Theodoret is saying he spoke Syriac *and* had a rustic background, indicating surely

---

6. Canivet 1977, 235. Festugière (1959, 291) begins his chapter entitled "Traits caractéristiques de l'anachorétisme syrien" with: "C'étaient généralement des gens simples souvent illettrés, ne parlant que le syriaque, ignorant le grec."

7. Ste. Croix makes a similar comment about the twentieth century, remarking that a sociological study in the 1950s showed that of 2,489 known Roman Catholic saints only 5 percent came from the lower classes (1981, 27).

8. See Browning 1981; and Patlagean 1983, 103. Fowden remarks that most pagan holy men were also from prosperous backgrounds (1982, 49).

9. *Life of Hilarion* 3; *Life of Paul of Thebes* 4; *Life of Malchus* 3; *Life of Martin of Tours*, preface; *Lausiac History* 46; *Life of John the Almsgiver* 2; *Life of Benedict*, prologue. Gregory the Great makes a rather uncomfortable statement in this regard: "However, as often happens, nobility of family brings with it inferiority of soul" (*Life of Benedict* 23.2). The predilection for the upper classes is pervasive. Sulpicius Severus, describing the eighty monks who followed Martin when he fled from the mass of his followers, comments that there were many noblemen among them and that several became bishops (*Life of Martin of Tours* 10.5, 8). See Bowersock 2000, 264–65, on the vast wealth Rabbula gave up on the occasion of his baptism.

10. Browning (1981, 127) argues that since his mother later married someone important in the village he is not an exception and notes also that his father was well known (*Life of Theodore of Sykeon* 3, 25), but I still think that being the son of a prostitute and a circus acrobat is pretty damning in most circles.

that the two are not inextricably linked.[11] Third, there is Symeon, who had been a shepherd (26.1).[12] By contrast, eight (possibly ten) of the subjects are plainly described as being from distinguished families.[13] He may have wished to show what these people had sacrificed since such renunciation in itself is a criticism of society. It has to be said, however, that apart from the details of some of these well-connected holy men Theodoret does not concentrate on the aspect of a retreat to the desert as a criticism of society. In his case, a likely explanation is that he wished some of his holy men at least to be of the same social class as his readers so that the latter would take note.[14]

There is Marcianus, who, "despising both the distinction of his family (for he was of noble descent) and an illustrious position at court," abandoned his advantages to become a recluse (*Religious History* 3.2). Similarly, Publius, a member of the curial order and from a good family, gave away his inheritance to live a pious life (5.1). Theodoret tells us explicitly that both men were good looking, an attribute not ascribed to anyone else except Maris, for whom it is raised to stress his chastity. Even though Maris, being physically beautiful, had attended many festivals of martyrs he was still a virgin, a detail that perhaps is remarkably revealing about one aspect of such occasions (20.2).[15] Aphrahat, we learn, although he was a Persian, came from a distinguished and illustrious family (8.1), and Theodosius was distinguished for the luster of his family (10.1). Zeno renounced exceptionally plentiful wealth in the Pontus as well as a post in the imperial service in order to live in solitude (12.1). Theo-

11. Language is discussed later in this chapter. See Rubenson 2000 on the attitude toward education, or the lack of it, among Christian biographers.

12. Price (1985a, 173, n. 3) asserts that the detail that Symeon had been a shepherd was "doubtless a typological accretion" since the *Life of Symeon* (11), written in Syriac by an anonymous author (in Doran 1992, 103–98) mentions his very wealthy aunt. Price's view supports the impression one gets from saints' lives that while the authors wish their subjects to be humble very often they came from prosperous backgrounds. We know from John Chrysostom that Julian Saba was from a poor background, but Theodoret does not tell us this. See Festugière 1959, 291 (John Chrysostom, Homily 21 on Ephesians).

13. Rousseau (1998, 234) and Price (1985a, xxxvi) also mention Asterius as being of the upper classes (*Religious History* 2.7), but I have not listed him here as he is not the subject of a life.

14. Browning (1981, 127) observes that poverty is not a moral category unless it is voluntary and also points to the snob value of wellborn heroes.

15. Antony is also stunningly good-looking (*Life of Antony* 14), presumably because he too was wellborn. Theodoret does not tell us that any of his heroes were ugly, although Sabinus, a disciple of Marcianus, is described as "ruddy with spots on his face" (*Religious History* 3.22).

doret tells us that Marana and Cyra were from stock that was the glory of their fatherland (29.2) and that Domnina's relatives were likewise not poor (30.3). A ninth, Abraham, clearly had good connections since his friends lent him a hundred gold pieces to clear a village's debts (17.3), and this might indicate high social status on his part. If this were the case, it would be interesting since we also learn that he did not understand Greek (17.9) and normally one might assume that this ignorance indicated a lowly origin. Theodoret implies that Jacob of Cyrrhestica was of the upper class when he says "Nor are other men who have had a respectable upbringing ready to evacuate excrement in the presence of strangers" (21.5.).

Canivet discusses the nomenclature of the holy men in his chapter on social origins but remarks that names, as illustrated in the case of Macedonius, can be confusing rather than enlightening.[16] Thalelaeus, the possessor of a Greek name, surprised Theodoret by speaking Greek, the assumption being that normally holy men spoke Syriac. This man, explains Theodoret, was Cilician, hence his Greek (*Religious History* 28.4). A knowledge of Syriac by itself was not a sign of humble birth. Theodoret knew this (21.15), and so did many upper-class people in the east.[17] It may be that all the ascetics, apart from the seven just mentioned, were from humble backgrounds and that Theodoret comments only on the exceptions. However, he is not explicit about this and this in itself is noteworthy. It is at least possible that Theodoret, who is after all writing in a literary style in classical Greek, was reassuring his readers that these Syrian ascetics were men of value, not merely ignorant peasants who knew no better. Certainly only educated people could read the *Religious History,*

---

16. Canivet 1977, 247–48. In this chapter, entitled "Origine sociale et culture des moines" (235–53), Canivet surveys the origins of the names, Semitic, Greek, and Latin, and comments that the proportion of noble to humble among the figures in the *Religious History* is probably in inverse proportion to the real situation since Theodoret is often focusing on the leaders who would tend to come from upper-class backgrounds (251).

17. Hilarion also spoke it as well as Greek (*Life of Hilarion* 22). This is an interesting case: one of the emperor's assistants from France was possessed by a demon and asked for a travel permit to see the holy man in Palestine to be freed from it. He spoke only French and Latin, but the demon replied to Hilarion in Syriac because that was the language in which he was addressed. So that the man's interpreters could understand, Hilarion also spoke to it in Greek. The issue of language is important in the *Life of Daniel the Stylite,* where it is mentioned to stress Daniel's origins and what can happen when people do not understand (see chaps. 10, 14, 17). Cf. Sozomen, *Ecclesiastical History* 3.16, on Ephraim's works being translated into Greek.

and it is striking how often Theodoret mentions members of the upper classes among his subjects as well as among the recipients of benefits performed by the aforesaid individuals. He says specifically that Symeon Stylites would talk to anyone, whatever their status, but goes on to list only craftsmen, beggars, and peasants, as if one might find this exceptional (26.25).

Language

If language is not a reliable indicator of social class, what does it tell us? Theodoret is careful to inform the reader about the languages used by his holy men.[18] The first instance is from the life of Eusebius (*Religious History* 4.13). Here he says that the monks whom Eusebius taught went out to establish their own schools, which can be found in the west and the south, praising God, some in Greek and some in what he calls the local language, which he does not specify (4.13). The emphasis is on the fact that it is not all in Greek, and we can see something similar in the next life, that of Publius, who is from the curial order. Although Theodoret does not say so explicitly, he must have been a Greek speaker since we are told that he had some followers who worshiped with him in Greek. Some Syriac speakers begged to be allowed to join him, and after Publius's death the two communities had different leaders, Theotecnus for the Greeks and Aphthonius for the Syriac speakers. This might imply that Publius himself spoke both languages since during his lifetime he was the sole leader (5.5–6). Aphthonius may have been bilingual since he has a Greek name, but this is not certain since Macedonius, another bearer of a Greek name, did not understand the language (13.7).

Theodoret himself comments at the beginning of the fourth life, that of Eusebius, that he has described men who lived in the desert and now is moving on to those who lived in populated areas. This is not entirely accurate since the first, Jacob, was bishop of Nisibis, which must count as a populated area.[19] However, this is his description, and he then gives us the lives of Eusebius and Publius, commenting explicitly on language in both lives. In other words,

18. Theodoret's references to Greek and Syriac in the *Religious History* are also discussed in Urbainczyk 2000.

19. This is discussed in Rousseau 1998, 240.

when moving on to those who live in the wider society, Theodoret comments on language, informing the reader that there were communities of Syriac-speaking monks as well as Greek-speaking ones. Arrangements were made to accommodate people who could not speak Greek. There is no mention of any attempt to teach them Greek.[20]

Theodoret raises the issue of language in the life of Macedonius, who is extremely important in the *Religious History,* being, in some sense Theodoret's spiritual father (*Religious History* 13).[21] It is through his intercession that Theodoret's parents produce their son. The story of the birth is the climax of the life, which holds a prominent place in the work, as he is the last of those from the region of Antioch, that is, he is not from Cyrrhus. Theodoret explicitly says that Macedonius was very famous and in the final paragraph stresses his importance by listing the important people who attended his funeral. There is an episode, which Theodoret says he is repeating in order to illustrate his hero's simplicity and innocence, in which Flavian, the bishop of Antioch at the time, tricked Macedonius into being ordained. When the holy man realized what had happened he chased the offending bishop with a stick. This story occurs early on (13.4) so that the reader will understand that this man is supposed to be rather unworldly, but it is not until three paragraphs later that we learn that he only spoke Syriac and that this presumably is why he did not understand what was going on.

The passage previous to this is the one quoted at the beginning of this chapter, wherein, during the famous episode of the riot of statues in Antioch, Macedonius reproached two generals and told them to tell the emperor not to punish the city. Theodoret comments that his speech had to be translated into Greek for the generals because Macedonius spoke in Syriac. Theodoret carefully makes the point that someone with no Greek was giving instructions to the emperor himself. In the next sentence, in case the reader did not understand this, he says that the Holy Spirit must have put the words into the holy man's mouth since the man had had no education and only a

---

20. Brock (1994, 158) mentions the establishment of Publius's two communities as the resolution of a problem.

21. Macedonius is unique in having a Greek name but not knowing Greek (Canivet 1977, 248). Individuals who do not speak Greek usually have Aramaic names or ones derived from the Old or New Testaments.

rustic upbringing but nevertheless could be eloquent. Speaking Syriac here is closely linked to having no education.

The next holy man in the text is Maësymas, and Theodoret comments that he is now describing ascetics from Cyrrhus (*Religious History* 14.1). As was noted earlier, Maësymas is described as speaking Syriac, having had a rustic upbringing, and being very virtuous. His life, or rather Theodoret's account of it, is very short, only five paragraphs long. It is surely significant that the largest proportion of it is again an example of defiance, of standing up to those in authority. Authority here is represented by a member of the council of Antioch, a certain Letoius, who was behaving tyrannically toward the village. Maësymas urged him to show kindness and when he was snubbed cursed him so that his carriage would not move.[22] Letoius had to fall at the holy man's feet before he would lift his curse and allow him to continue on his way. Again, being a Syriac speaker is a way of emphasizing lowly origins, which are being used to show the enormous power and influence such a person could achieve through his devotion to God.

Abraham is a similar case. He was also born and brought up in Cyrrhus, although he goes to the Lebanon and saves some of its inhabitants from impiety by lending some villagers money for their taxes. The money was not his personally; he was helped by some of his friends. He is therefore not without influence, although Theodoret does not explain how he won it.[23] Abraham is later made bishop of Carrhae and continues to live ascetically while carrying out his duties such as judging lawsuits. Theodoret comments that even the emperor wanted to see him and sent for him. "A choir" of empresses clasped his hands and knees and made supplication to a man who did not even understand Greek (*Religious History* 17.9). Again the contrast is between high and low, and to emphasize it Theodoret uses language. The man did not even know Greek. In the next paragraph Theodoret describes a funeral even more elaborate than that of Macedonius. A report on the funeral of an ascetic is not a regular occurrence in the *Religious History*. However, here there is

---

22. See Trombley's reconstruction of these events as an excellent example of the way in which Theodoret's account is shamelessly ravaged for a narrative acceptable to modern historians (1995, 162–63).

23. Canivet observes that Theodoret never describes holy men who have an Aramaic or biblical name as being from a distinguished family, except for Aphrahat, who was a Persian (1977, 248).

a careful description of all the important people who attended, civilians, soldiers, subjects, governors, empresses, and the emperor himself. An individual is thus elevated to a position where he is paid respect by the emperor. His humble origins make him even more remarkable (13.8).

On one occasion, Syriac is spoken not by an ascetic but by a demon. This episode occurs in the life of Jacob of Cyrrhestica, who receives the longest account of the work and is the first of the living holy men, just as the life of Jacob of Nisibis opened the whole work (Theodoret himself comments on the symmetry of the names). Theodoret plays a large role in this life, as is discussed later, and in this particular episode we learn that Marcionites were causing trouble in Cyrrhus. Theodoret was doing his best to get rid of these heretics when one night a wicked demon came and roared at him in Syriac to stop his warring against Marcion. The demon added that he would have destroyed Theodoret long ago if he had not seen a choir of martyrs with Jacob protecting him (*Religious History* 21.15). It could be that the devil spoke Syriac because that is the language people spoke in Cyrrhus, but Theodoret does not note every time someone speaks in Cyrrhus that they were speaking Syriac.[24] More likely, this attribution of language is meant to emphasize the threat posed by the forces of evil since they communicate directly with the masses.[25] Theodoret, too, can do this, but he fights on God's side. He tells the reader that the demon spoke Syriac to him, that he heard and understood, and that his companions did, too.[26]

A slightly different, but equally important, passage occurs in a very short life presented toward the end of the whole work, that of Thalelaeus, mentioned earlier. This holy man is rather odd — his speciality in terms of asceticism was an elaborate device that consisted of

24. Canivet and Leroy-Molinghen suggest this (1977–79, 95, n. 3). Brock (1994, 154) uses the story to argue that Syriac was Theodoret's mother tongue. On this topic, see chapter 1.

25. Sobré (1987), discussing a work by Vincent Ferrer from the fourteenth century in which God speaks Latin and Satan the vernacular, argues that this attribution of language is intended to show that people need priests to intercede with God but Satan is much more accessible.

26. The mention of demons recalls the Messalians since they had the curious notion that everyone is possessed by a demon, or sin, which has to be eradicated by means of prayer. Theodoret shows little interest in these views in the *Religious History,* for which see his *Ecclesiastical History* (4.11). See also Canivet 1961, Murray 1975, and Stewart 1991.

two connected wheels. He suspended himself in this contraption, which kept him bent double, so that he could not straighten his neck but had to keep his forehead tightly pressed against his knees. When Theodoret wrote his description of this ascetic, Thalelaeus had been squashed in this device for ten years. Apart from this strange practice and the reason why he did it, which was that he thought by punishing himself now he could reduce his punishment in the afterlife, very little information about him is provided. But one crucial detail Theodoret provides is that this man spoke Greek. Theodoret asked him why he was tormenting himself in this way and reports that the ascetic replied in Greek, for he happened to be Cilician by race.[27]

This passage leads us to infer that most of the people whom Theodoret describes spoke in Syriac. He wants to remind the reader of this fact by giving the information late in the work, in the twenty-eighth life. He is drawing attention to the fact that these are not educated men, not men of the upper classes, but more remarkable for being of native stock. In other words, there is a tension in his work. Although when he is specific about the social level of his ascetics' background he more often than not describes them as wealthy, he also wants to give the impression that most of his heroes are the dispossessed. After all, it was not difficult for educated men to think up clever arguments, gain power, and influence people. It was almost unheard of for uneducated people to do so before the advent of Christianity. And even within Christian circles well-connected people, as is only to be expected, held the positions of power. This contradiction is thus observed even in Theodoret's own work since he stresses the lowly origins of his heroes while also wishing to describe those who had given up their wealth to join the ranks of the humble when he comments that eight of them had done so.

It is probable that most monks in Syria were of humble origin and spoke Syriac. It is also likely that those who founded monasteries were more likely to come from privileged backgrounds than ordinary ascetics and thus more likely to speak Greek.[28] This means that we

---

27. *Religious History* 28.4. See also Holl 1908 and MacMullen 1966. Jones (1964, 994) has the more obvious interpretation of this passage (see Hopwood 1994, 344). Trombley (1995, 160–61) has a perverse interpretation of this passage. He says that since Thalelaeus did not know Syriac he compensated with his extreme asceticism: "If words were insufficient to convert the rustics, perhaps actions might" (161).

28. Canivet 1977, 251. See also Bagnall 1993, 301–2, for a similar situation in Egypt.

receive an unrepresentative cross section from the *Religious History* because Theodoret tends to mention those who founded communities rather than ordinary members. In other words, in reality the proportion of Greek to Syriac was probably smaller than is presented in the *Religious History*. The passage about Thalelaeus supports this. Theodoret is trying to make his holy men as spectacular as possible, and he also knows those for whom he is writing and what their preconceptions would be, probably because he holds them himself. To speak only Syriac is a sign of a lack of education, of being one of the peasants, and Theodoret wishes to show that he has support from such people, who make up the mass of the inhabitants of the area. Thus, there will be trouble if he is deposed. John Chrysostom had been recalled due to popular demand.

Speaking Syriac indicates nothing about social status in itself. After all, Theodoret spoke it. It is the lack of Greek that is the indicator. This is illustrated most clearly by the eighth life, that of Aphrahat, who was a Persian. The attitudes revealed in this life are striking. Apparently Aphrahat despised his family, although it was distinguished and illustrious, and went to live in Antioch. Although he only knew a few phrases of Greek, he drew vast numbers of people to him through his wisdom. Theodoret describes his language as semi-barbarous (*Religious History* 8.2). Presumably he learned Greek not Syriac because he lived in Antioch rather than its environs. In the next sentence Theodoret asked who had ever surpassed that uneducated barbarian voice, and he goes onto quote Paul, "Even if unskilled in speaking I am not unskilled in knowledge" (2 Cor 11.16), which neatly sums up Christian attitudes toward learning and wisdom.

Aphrahat's noble Persian background counts for nothing with the Greeks, and his ignorance of Greek means that he is an uneducated barbarian. His language is semibarbarian because he knows some phrases in Greek; otherwise it would be completely barbarian. Again Theodoret wishes to present his hero as existing outside the ruling class. As in the case of Abraham, who was able to raise a vast sum of money to help his village, Aphrahat was not a member of the Syrian masses. The image Theodoret wants to portray is that of an outsider. The ability to speak the language counts for almost everything, and yet the grace of God can make even a Persian superior to the emperor. Not all holy men in the *Religious History* address emperors, but Aphrahat does and he punishes an imperial eunuch for disrespect by having him boiled to death in a hot bath. He also cures one of the emperor's horses, although this did not deflect the emperor (Valens) from his impiety.

People who do not speak Greek are barbarians. It would seem that not much had changed from classical times. A lack of Greek is a sign of not belonging, of being an outsider, but this status in Christian eyes can be a token of distinction and becomes a topos in this kind of literature. Language identifies the holy men as exceptional. Their achievements become all the more remarkable because they start from nothing and therefore the power they reveal must be divine. It must be God putting words into their mouths because they are not educated, the implication being that without God the lower classes have nothing interesting to say. Theodoret emphasizes the lack of knowledge of Greek when he wishes to show a holy man having dealings with the court or with governors because not all do.

The individuals Theodoret includes in his collection are a mixture of noble and lowly. The leaders of communities are more likely to come from upper-class backgrounds since such people are more likely to assume a leadership role. Perhaps Theodoret wants his monks to be impressive and suitable, or perhaps realistic, models for the readers of Constantinople. Consequently he had to include some examples of the wealthy. In many respects, however, lower-class men, and even more so women of any class, are more impressive because they are unusual and unfamiliar to his readers. They also are more terrifying to contemplate since they are "the other" by definition. Such heroes are more central to Theodoret's concerns, and he emphasizes language to draw attention to their regional quality. Syriac speakers are from Syria. They belong there and have influence there. Their divine attributes bring benefits to their homeland. They are the troops available to the leaders in Syria. Bishops, that is, good bishops who have won their respect, can look to them for support.

Theodoret's purpose is not simply to show how anyone can defy the emperor if they have God on their side; he also uses the issue of language to associate himself with the Syriac speakers. Although he is originally from Antioch, he wants his readers to know that he belongs in this area of remote villages and strange ascetics. We see him talking to the holy men he particularly mentions as not knowing Greek, such as Macedonius (*Religious History* 13), and when the devil spoke to Theodoret he did so in Syriac (21.15). We see from the *Religious*

History that many Syrian ascetics did not speak Greek and consequently Theodoret's opponents, that is, clerics from Egypt, who, whatever their linguistic skills, did not speak Syriac, were suppose to realize that they could not win these people over to their side. Theodoret, on the other hand, spoke their language and had their loyalty and respect.

Chapter 6

The Desert and the City:
How the Holy Men Lived

Bidding farewell to all this [a position at court], he repaired to the heart of the desert, and built a small cell that was not even the size of his body. Surrounding it with another small wall, he was immured continuously and deprived of all human company, while conversing with the Master of the universe and hearkening to that sweet voice, for in reading the divine oracles he held he was enjoying the divine voice, and by praying and making supplication he conversed with the Master. (*Religious History* 3.2)

The *Religious History* is commonly viewed as a series of lives of solitary ascetics, individuals who withdrew physically from their local communities and very often from all human society. But, while in some sense this is true, it is not the full picture. Theodoret comments on how numerous monasteries were, and this is borne out by his text. In fact, there is not a single example of an ascetic who is utterly solitary and in many cases monasteries play a significant role in the life of the individual being described.[1] If the ascetics never mingled with anyone Theodoret would not know about them and so could not write about them, but, in describing the asceticism of his heroes, he could have omitted or ignored their interaction with others had he wished to portray them in complete isolation. What is interesting here is the mixture of so-called coenobitic and anchorite existences. The whole work bears out what Gould has drawn attention to, namely, that it is misleading to see these as exclusive alternatives since for many monks both were adopted at different stages of their

---

1. Canivet (1977, 2089–9) observes that we see Theodoret's holy men going from communal to solitary living and sometimes back again. Adnès and Canivet (1967, 58–60) remark that a dozen monks are heads of monasteries and that only two of these, Julian Saba and Marcianus, are reported to have performed miracles. See "Monachisme" in Viller, Cavallera, and de Guibert 1980, cols. 1524–71.

lives.[2] Rousseau has stressed that the community was always important even for eremitic or semi-eremitic individuals.[3]

Two lives in particular are relevant here, and interestingly it is those that were wrongly separated, namely, 22–23 and 24–25. It is not difficult to see why this separation occurred since they are different from the rest of the lives in that they describe several individuals. The relationship between the ascetics in them is not altogether clear. Polychronius is the pupil of Zebinas, but Asclepius is simply described as being "of this company" (*Religious History* 24–25). Similarly, Limnaeus was a pupil of Maron but seems to have lived near or with Thalassius since he is described as "in his choir" (22.3). Limnaeus built a monastery for his followers of blind beggars, throwing startling light on the apparent number of blind people there were in the area (22.7). Theodoret also adds John, Moses, Antiochus, and Antoninus to this account and Jacob of Nimouza to the next one (25). It is as if he suddenly became tired and just started to list individuals. But the reason for the clusters in these chapters is presumably that they were in the same geographical area. In both chapters we have villages that remain unidentified today (Tillima and Cittica), but it would appear that several are connected by a teacher-pupil relationship and, as might be expected, some of the pupils stayed close to their teachers.

In some cases the ascetic is merely interacting with clerics or the laity or both, as Jacob of Nisibis does. His intercourse with the wider world is the most spectacular in the *Religious History* since he not only slew the arch-heretic Arius with his tongue (1.10) but turned back the whole Persian army from the walls of Nisibis, this time using mosquitoes (1.11–13). Some holy men are also priests or bishops, such as Maësymas or Abraham (14, 17), and thus automatically have dealings with their local communities. One of the holy women spends much time praying and weeping but practices "other forms of virtue" as well, such as ministering to holy men, looking after visitors, and sending food to Theodoret (30.3). Many holy men must have had friends who visited regularly with food and to make sure they were all right. In the life of Zeno we are told that his friends supplied him with food and books (12.3, 5). Even though Theodoret

2. See Gould 1993, esp. 88–106; see also 17, 139.
3. Rousseau 1978, 34. Likewise, pagan holy men sought solitude but not total isolation (Fowden 1982, 56–58).

only describes his own interaction with Maris, at the beginning of the life he tells us that this holy man lived in a village called Omeros (20.1). Thus, although one aspect of asceticism was a solitary life, one should not interpret this as absolute solitude, at least from a reading of the *Religious History*.

In many instances, there is much more human contact than in the examples just cited. Even when the individual wished for solitude, he was often pursued by admirers or those needing help. Romanus receives only a very brief account, but in it we learn that he cured many of serious diseases and helped the childless conceive (*Religious History* 11.4). Indeed, in the previous paragraph Theodoret says that "he did not enjoy these labors in solitude," although it is not entirely clear whether he means that others came to visit or actually lived with him (11.3). Maron also healed his visitors of physical ailments, but in addition, remarkably perhaps, he cured anger, greed, intemperance, and sloth as well as teaching self-control and justice (16.3). Similarly, we know that Baradatus and Thalelaeus were not always alone when we hear about the people they helped (27.3, 28.5). Some holy men were friends and thus must have communicated, such as Palladius, Symeon the Elder, and a man called Abraham (7.1, 4). Jacob of Cyrrhestica was a companion of Maron, we are told (21.3), and the famous Peter the Galatian had as a companion, Daniel, a man who had come to him to get rid of his demon (9.4).

Some guests were more welcome than others. Even Acepsimas, who is one of the closest, as far as one can tell, to leading a completely solitary life in that Theodoret says he spent "sixty years neither being seen nor speaking," did not escape (*Religious History* 15.1). He was tormented by a visitor (not Theodoret) who climbed a nearby tree so that he could spy on the holy man (15.3). The miscreant was punished with paralysis, which only disappeared when the tree was cut down.[4] Salamanes was kidnapped by his admirers

---

4. Punishments provide entertaining reading, but again we find that this was not Theodoret's main purpose, and there are not as many episodes in the *Religious History* as we find in other lives. For instance, in the *Life of Benedict* we hear that seven naked girls were sent by a priest to tempt the monks. The priest was punished by having a building collapse on him, killing him (*Life of Benedict* 4). In the same life we hear of a very young monk, in fact still a little boy, who, because he missed his parents, went to visit them without permission and died (as a consequence of his disobedience) on the same day. He would not even stay buried until Benedict had blessed him (24.2). Jerome (in his *Life of Hilarion* 34) says about the consequences of wrongdoing: "In this connection, as there is

(19.3), and Macedonius moved several times, not because he did not like where he lived but because he was trying to escape from the people who flocked to him (13.2). Symeon also fled his admirers, barbarians in his case (6.4). Eusebius of Asikha felt so oppressed by his callers that he escaped to the nearest community of ascetics and lived there, thus offering an insight into one of the advantages of the communal life (18.3).[5] Antony provides a famous precedent for this flight, as he also tried to escape those who flocked round him (*Life of Antony* 44, 49).[6]

In the majority of the lives we see the ascetics living for at least a while in a community with like-minded people. The life of Julian Saba is replete with references to those who came to emulate his way of life. He had so many disciples that he tried to escape them by setting out for Mount Sinai, but even so he took some close companions with him (*Religious History* 2.13). Marcianus initially lived with two others, who in turn had their own communities, numbering more than four hundred souls by Theodoret's time (3.4). He ends the account by describing some of Marcianus's disciples, Eusebius, Basil, and Sabinus (3.19, 20, 21), commenting, "I have made this digression wishing to show for how many others the great Marcianus was the cause of great achievements" (3.19). This ties in with Theodoret's purpose for his whole work, that is, that others will observe these models of piety and wish to emulate them. One might almost see Theodoret's *Religious History* as a monastery, a collection of individuals, to which readers come to learn.

The fourth life of the *Religious History* is extremely important in this respect because so many followers are mentioned. Perhaps one of the most significant speeches of the whole work appears here. Eusebius had lived in complete isolation, not speaking to anyone or

---

no other opportunity to tell it, I would only mention this (so as to inspire fear in those who fail to respect their masters): shortly afterward this man caught leprosy and rotted away."

5. See Canivet 1977, 213, on the structure of these monasteries and the wall that often encircled them.

6. Hilarion also wished to escape his followers. Jerome describes them thus: "Bishops and priests, flocks of clerics and monks used to throng to him, as did large numbers of Christian women (a great temptation), as well as crowds of common people from every direction, from cities and from the countryside." Hilarion was prevented from leaving by more than ten thousand such people (*Life of Hilarion* 30). One cannot help feeling that often Jerome is simply trying to make his readers laugh. Martin of Tours was another who tried to escape his admirers. He fled with eighty others. So for him eighty companions was solitude! (*Life of Martin of Tours* 10.3).

even going outside, and would have gone to his death in this fashion had not another ascetic, Ammianus, asked him whom he thought he was pleasing by living such an austere life. When he replied, naturally, God, the other remarked that

> "Restricting all one's care to oneself would not escape, I think, the charge of self-love, for the divine law prescribes loving one's neighbor as oneself. . . . So, since you too are a fervent lover of the God who has created and saved, make many others as well his lovers.". . . With these and like words he charmed the divine man; digging through his voluntary prison, he led him out and away, and entrusted to him care of the brethren. (4.4)

There is no sense of anything but complete approval for Ammianus's words to Eusebius on the part of Theodoret. It is rather a strange speech to find in a work celebrating what we might think of as the typical Syrian ascetic, but it is thoroughly in keeping with other sentiments we find in this work, which was after all written by a bishop. After this, one reads the comment on the life of Maris rather differently: "but living like recluses he looked after his own soul and then increased his virtue through the labors of reclusion" (20.2). One cannot help feeling that there is a little reproach here. And perhaps it should be noted that Maris receives a much shorter account than Eusebius. Macedonius told Theodoret's mother that self-starvation was not a virtue (13.3). Bassus told Symeon that suicide was the greatest crime (26.7), and in the life of Eusebius it is difficult not to read Ammianus's statement as a criticism of complete withdrawal. One has a wider duty, in Theodoret's eyes, to other people. And it is presumably because of this view that we find such an emphasis on communities in the work; it is not simply a record of individual stars. This is in direct contrast to the sentiment found in the *Life of Antony,* where the holy man is reported to have said that monks in society are like fish on dry land (85).

Publius, the subject of the next life, attracted many others to a pious life by his example (*Religious History* 5.3), and we learn about the communities that grew up around him.[7] At first the followers

---

7. Theodoret says that Publius actually trapped followers and compares him to a singing bird used as bait. He says that he drew many of his fellows into this trap of salvation (*Religious History* 5.3). In the life of Eusebius he says that Marianus ensnared

lived in individual cells, and later Publius agreed to one large building for all of them.[8] Most of this life is in fact about the men the
master inspired rather than Publius himself, and Theodoret himself
comments on this, saying:

> Such is what I have learnt of the great Publius — of which some
> came to me by hearsay and some by my seeing his disciples, recog-
> nizing the teacher in his disciples and discovering the trainer
> through his athletes. (5.10)

Here Theodoret uses two images that are important for the *Religious
History,* those of the philosophical school and athletics.[9] As we have
seen, in the first line of the prologue Theodoret refers to his ascetics
as athletes of virtue and uses the metaphor constantly.[10] As in the
passage cited, the picture of the philosophic school is also never far
away and sometimes they mingle, as when Theodoret describes Julian's followers as athletes of philosophy (2.9).[11] Rousseau suggests
that the role of teaching in asceticism was central and that ascetics
saw themselves primarily as teachers.[12] Thus, the imagery of a coach
training his athletes and a master instructing his pupils is apt. This
may seem to be an unusual interpretation, but on closer inspection it
would appear to be indisputable since, if it is about anything, Christianity must be about teaching the Word of God. The evangelical
aspect is fundamental and evident in Theodoret's work, which, as
noted earlier, is itself designed to teach, to offer models for others to
follow. To be truly virtuous one had to be useful, and this meant
bringing others to God or teaching them how to approach Him. One
could do this within or without a religious community, but there was

---

Eusebius and his brother (4.3). See also 2.3 for similar language. Jerome says that as a
result of Hilarion's example countless monasteries sprang up round Palestine (*Life of
Hilarion* 24).

8. See Canivet (1977, 212) on the nature of this building.

9. This is discussed at length by Rousseau (1998, esp. 235–37).

10. See, for example, *Religious History* 2.3, 2.9, 3.5, 4.2, and 9.12.

11. See, for example, ibid., 2.6, 3.4, and 8.2. For more examples and a discussion,
see Rousseau 1998.

12. "In the matter of identity, that was what asceticism was for: to prepare oneself to
teach, and to fulfill the task effectively. We have to distinguish between teaching that took
place within ascetic groups and teaching that was directed beyond them; but, while the first
was regarded as primary, the second was a natural, even if dependent extension." (Rousseau 1998, 231).

often a community involved at some point in an ascetic's life. Julian, Publius, and Theodosius, for instance, all left solitude to live with others (2.4, 5.2, 10.2).[13]

The master-pupil relationship is portrayed frequently in the *Religious History*.[14] We learn that Maron, for instance,

> produced many plants of philosophy, and it was he who planted for God the garden that now flourishes in the region of Cyrrhus. A product of his planting was the great James. (16.3)

In many of the lives Theodoret comments on those who carried on the work begun by their teacher. In the case of Julian Saba we learn that people flocked to learn from him, but Theodoret also describes the holy man as ensnaring his fellow men.

> For not only do birds catch other birds through calling to themselves by song those of the same species and entangling them in snares laid around, but men also entrap their fellow-men, sometimes for their harm, sometimes for their salvation. (2.3)

And eventually he had a hundred followers.[15] Similarly, Theodosius attracted many whom he organized into work forces, with some making sails, hair coats, or mats or engaging in farming (10.3).[16] In other cases Theodoret simply picks out one pupil to describe, such as Marcianus, Sabinus (3.21), or Thalassius (with his famous pupil, Limnaeus, who dominates life 22–23). Theodoret also singles out Jacob (of Cyrrhestica, the subject of life 21) as the pupil of Maron, who in turn may have been made the subject of a life because of this fact since we learn little else about him (16.3). Zebinas taught the great Polychronius, who was, we learn, as like his master as wax is like the seal (24.3). In turn Asclepius was part of this community before he went to join the Teleda school (25.1).

---

13. See Canivet 1977, 184–85, on the manual labor in Theodosius's monastery.

14. On this, see Rousseau 1998 and Rousseau 2000 on Antony in particular. See MacDermot 1971, 29, on the importance of the master-disciple relationship in early asceticism, when the community was seen as a training ground for the life of a hermit.

15. See also *Religious History* 11.3 for the general comment that Romanus inspired many with his way of life.

16. This organization is unusual, or rather Theodoret's description is, in that he seldom gives so many details on the lives of these communities.

When Eusebius of Teleda died Theodoret remarked that offshoots of his philosophy could be seen in the west and the south, praising God in Greek or Syriac (*Religious History* 4.13). In the following life he again comments on the use of the two languages among the disciples of Publius (5.6). Symeon the Elder established two communities, one at the top of a mountain and the other at its foot, and trained his followers in both (6.13). Marana and Cyra had their community of maidservants (29.2), and Bassus was the head of a group of more than two hundred disciples (26.8). The great Symeon himself joins a group of ascetics temporarily, from which he is expelled for his extreme behavior, although they continue to feel responsible for him and retrieve him from a deep cistern (26.4–6). Teaching similarly was of central importance in the Egyptian communities, as Gould points out.[17] One can see a parallel with the biographies of philosophers, in which it was important to mention a man's followers since in large part the subject was judged by their quality and number.[18]

No ascetic is portrayed as completely isolated. They all have dealings with other people; they are visited by admirers and followers, some of whom stay. Throughout the *Religious History* there are references to numerous communities that the ascetics found, visit, or leave. Interaction with others is the medium through which their holiness is perceived; their miracles are corroborations of their teachings, and all miracles require witnesses. The communities are the schools where Theodoret's heroes are taught or teach. They may follow examples or set them, but the continuation is vital.

The number of individuals is huge, but so also is the number of communities. In the last life, that of Domnina, he says:

Myriad and defeating enumeration are the philosophic retreats of this kind not only in our region but throughout the East; full of them are Palestine, Egypt, Asia, Pontus, and all Europe. (*Religious History* 30.5)

And he repeats himself in the following chapter, with perhaps a proviso.

---

17. Gould 1993, 27–33.
18. Cox 1983, 24.

As I have said, numerous are the pious wrestling-schools of men and women not only among us but also in all Syria, Palestine, Cilicia, and Mesopotamia. In Egypt, it is said, some retreats have five thousand men each. (30.6)

Reasonably enough, he seems to find the figures quoted for the monasteries in Egypt extremely large, but he does mention them to support his picture of vast numbers of monks all over the eastern part of the empire. And he ends his whole account with the communities, not the individuals.

Chapter 7

Miracles and Marvels:
What the Holy Men Did

Some living in tents and others in cells chant hymns to God; others embrace the life in holes and caves. Many, of whom I have recalled some, have not been induced to have a cave or hole or hut or cell, but giving their bodies to the naked air endure contrasts of temperature, sometimes frozen by unrelieved frost, sometimes burnt by the fire of the sun's rays. Of these again the life is various: some stand all the time, others divide the day between sitting and standing; some, immured in enclosures, shun the company of the many; others, with no such covering, are exposed to all who wish to see them. (*Religious History* 27.1)

Theodoret starts his life of Baradatus with this survey of the variety of ascetic practices he has come across in Syria and which he has described for his readers. In his prologue he explained that he was giving a series of accounts because his subjects were all different (8). In some sense what Theodoret, and to a larger extent the authors of the Egyptian works, presented in their texts was a freak show. Strange individuals, who lived in ways most people found disagreeable, were being paraded to ordinary mortals for their entertainment and edification.[1]

"Where did all this madness come from?" asked E. R. Dodds when he was faced with this asceticism.[2] Some may find this response anachronistic and unsympathetic to the ancient mind, but it should be remembered that contemporary readers were expected by the authors to have a similar reaction. There are frequent assurances in the works

---

1. "In Syria and Mesopotamia asceticism occasionally took bizarre forms. The majority of monks were very simple Syriac-speaking people, ignorant of Greek. Their recorded mortifications make alarming reading" (Chadwick 1967, 180).

2. Dodds 1965, 34.

that these stories may seem incredible but are true, and authors include explanations as to why humans felt the need to behave in this strange way. For the pagan antecedents such as the Cynics much of their influence came precisely from their ability to shock. The holy men not only behaved oddly but they were able to perform miracles, which, by definition, were events to be marveled at. One of the most startling examples is that of Marcianus, who had a light flashing from his head, enabling him to read (*Religious History* 3.6).

Theodoret relates his lives with less sensational stories than one finds in other works. There are, for instance, fewer miracles in the *Religious History,* though they do occur. Most interestingly, they are clustered in the lives of those holy men with the closest connection to Theodoret himself, thus reinforcing the argument that the work was meant to buttress his own position. The reader, having been presented with a more muted picture than we find elsewhere, nevertheless comes away from the text amazed at its contents. These are no ordinary individuals described therein. Theodoret is conscious of this and sometimes comments on it. From the level of the Greek we know that he is writing for a more sophisticated audience than the one for whom the *History of the Monks of Egypt* was accessible. Thus, his options are more limited in the type of event he can narrate, but he clearly wants to give the impression that what the reader will encounter is almost incredible. By describing the ascetics as deferential to the church, and especially to himself, he informs anyone who cares to know that these are loyal allies who will help him and the Syrian church in any struggle. What kind of allies does he present to the reader?

Richard Price, in the introduction to his translation of the *Religious History,* observes:

> The defect of the work is that it is magnificent as a series of stories, but feeble as a series of portraits. Theodoret's holy men are insufficiently differentiated, to the point where most of the stories, accidental details aside, would equally fit most of his holy men. It is the same ideal of saintliness that is reiterated again and again; and monotony is accentuated by the tone of panegyric, with its rigorous refusal to attribute to any of the holy men defects or limitations.[3]

---

3. Price 1985a, xv.

Price's judgment is not without foundation, although Theodoret had not exactly misrepresented his work. It is certainly true that Theodoret describes a wide variety of ascetic practices and activities. One carries heavy chains (*Religious History* 10.2), another walls himself up in a cell too small for him (3.2; see also 18.2), a third lies comatose and responds to nothing (19), while some stand all night (24.4) or live on a column (26).[4] There are two who imprison themselves, one in a box smaller than he was tall, the other suspended in a cage in which he cannot sit up straight (27, 28).

While all asceticism has some similarity, such as eating and sleeping very little,[5] often praying for long periods, and remaining chaste, Theodoret introduces diversity in the miracles the monks perform: one is brought dates by a lion (6.10);[6] another divines the identity of a murderer (7.2); and another punishes an imperial eunuch, who dies in a hot bath, and cures the emperor's horse (8.9, 11). Macedonius, upon learning of the riot of the statues in 387, rushes to save the city and rebukes the emperor (perhaps not a miracle but a remarkable occurrence in the ancient world [13.7]), and Maësymas clamps the wheels of a senator until he agrees to stop his unreasonable tax demands (14.4). Jacob of Nisibis drives back the army of the marauding Persians with his own army of mosquitoes, and Jacob of Cyrrhestica brings a child back to life (21.14).

Nevertheless, in an important sense Price is right. One does not come away with a strong sense of the individuality of these people. One character who does remain firmly in the reader's mind, however, is Theodoret. Yet he has achieved this limelight dexterously and rather stealthily, and it is a tribute to his ability that for the most part this has remained unobserved. Like all true artists, Theodoret does not reveal his skill. Also unobserved is the fact that for the most part the ascetics who perform the most miracles are those with the closest association with Theodoret.

---

4. Elliott (1987, 107) observes that Marcianus's cramped cell was rather like being in a womb in that the occupant had to curl up in this enclosure, which only had a small window (*Religious History* 3.6). Baradatus's box, on the other hand, had broad openings to let in the sun and rain (27.2).

5. Ibid., 138, 140. Elliott comments that many desert hermits were vegetarians and the consumption of meat was related to urban society. Many only ate raw food, and the *Religious History* has several examples of this, for instance, Jacob of Nisibis (1.2), Symeon the Elder (6.1), Macedonius (13.3), and Abraham (17.6). Romanus and Zeno also refuse to use fire (11.1, 12.2).

6. See Elliott 1987, 144–67, on the frequent rapport between saints and animals.

Miracles

How was it that his common sense took so different a line from
that of the skeptical minds of this day? What made him drink in
with such relish what we reject with such disgust? Was it that, at
least, some miracles were brought home so absolutely to his sen-
sible experience that he had no reason for doubting the others
which came to him second-hand? This certainly will explain what
to most of us is sure to seem the stupid credulity of so well-read, so
intellectual an author.[7]

This was Newman's response to the miracles in Theodoret's *Religious History,* which may seem rather surprising coming from a future cardinal. Modern scholars, however, have a tendency to think
that someone who wrote classical Greek should not be reporting on
miracles, let alone believing in them. One might be forgiven for
thinking that the *Religious History* is replete with supernatural occurrences, but this is not the case. As an example of hagiography, there
is relatively little of this aspect. It has been observed that Theodoret
himself is rarely an eyewitness to any of these incidents and that most
of the more dramatic miracles were performed by ascetics of the
past, those who had died before Theodoret wrote.[8] One might wish
to interpret this as Theodoret distancing himself from these events
but feeling obliged to include them because they are customary in
this literary genre.[9] It seems doubtful, however, that Theodoret allowed himself to be constrained by considerations of form, especially

7. Newman [1873] 1970, 2:314–15. A little later he comments: "Nothing was more
adapted to convert Orientals in that day than excesses of asceticism and anomalous displays of power, — manifestations, in short, which would shock and revolt an educated
European of the nineteenth century" (317). And, after describing a successful sermon, he
remarks, "It was much pleasanter thus to preach to sympathetic audiences than to be
stoned by a mob of brutal peasants on the Euphrates" (325).

8. Adnès and Canivet 1967, 60–64. Canivet (1977, 119) states that "une analyse
attentive prouve que les récits de miracles y sont relativement peu nombreux, si on la
compare aux oeuvres analogues." He also notes that Theodoret distinguishes between
illness and possession, (119), but that seems rather unsurprising since they are different.

9. Canivet 1977, 117–45. See Adnès and Canivet 1967 on healings and exorcisms.
See Canivet and Leroy-Molinghen 1977–79, 342–44, for a full list of the miracles. Binns
(1994, 223–24) discusses the categories of miracles. Van Uytfanghe (1981, 221) observes
that the earliest Christians viewed miracles as problematic, not that they occur at all but
that they can be misleading in various ways.

given the enormous potential of such events to influence his audience. He cannot but have been aware of this.

Canivet, in his study of miracles in the work, divides extraordinary events into "prodiges cosmiques" (achievements performed by only ten holy men such as punishing a man who pretended to be dead by killing him but then restoring him to life [1.10] or repelling locusts with blessed water [8.14]), healings, exorcisms, and prophecies (there are few of these). One should perhaps point out that there is no sense in which these events are categorized in this way in the text. By pointing out that most of the incidents are healings or exorcisms, which in turn could be described as a healing of the mind, Canivet appears to be trying to reduce the ascetics to rather effective doctors.[10]

However, when one considers Theodoret's own role in the work, the list of names of those who perform the most miracles leaps off the page since they are so familiar from an examination of the passages that deal with Theodoret or his family: Symeon (*Religious History* 6), Aphrahat (8), Peter (9), Macedonius (13), Jacob of Cyrrhestica (21), and Symeon Stylites (26).[11] Each of these has very strong associations with Theodoret. The first four are closely linked to his family, and the last two are perhaps the most important lives of the work since they are substantially longer than any others and Theodoret was very intimate with Jacob. Symeon had achieved great fame even during his own life, as was observed earlier, and his life may have been the culmination of the whole work.

It is therefore not so much the presence or lack of the miraculous in the *Religious History* that matters but its distribution. It should be

10. Canivet 1977, 127–28. Adnès and Canivet (1967, 67–82) argue that Theodoret's knowledge of medicine was not negligible. On the model of Christ as a doctor, see Canivet 1977, 127–30; and Adnès and Canivet 1967, 57.

11. Here I give the chapters devoted to miracles (I decided to count the chapters rather than the occurrences of miracles, as Theodoret sometimes speaks rather generally about them; see, e.g., 16.2 and Canivet and Leroy-Molinghen 1977–79, 342–44). In life 1 (Jacob of Nisibis) there are five chapters, life 2 has seven, and life 3 has four. There are none in lives 4 or 5, life 6 has four, life 7 has one, life 8 has four, and life 9 has seven. Life 10 is an interpolation; lives 11 and 12 have one each; life 13 has six; lives 14, 15, and 16 have two each; and there are none in lives 17, 18, 19, or 20. There is one in life 21, although there are several divine dreams and premonitions and much interaction with demons (and it should be said that the miracle is a resurrection [chap. 14, life 21]. There are none in lives 22–23, one in 24–25, four in 26, none in 27, one in 28, and none in 29 and 30.

acknowledged that miracles are also clustered in the first three lives of the work, those of Jacob of Nisibis, Julian Saba, and Marcianus. These ascetics have a rather special status, as they were already prominent figures in Syrian piety. They were the individuals furthest from Theodoret's own time, so their stories had had time to build up around them and their actions were well known and presumably often told. One would expect more miracles in these lives anyway.

Ascetics with a special relationship with Theodoret are those who perform the most wonders. One might also speculate whether this helps account for the relative scarcity of miracles in the work as a whole. If these individuals are to be marked as extraordinary they have to perform the most miracles, and if there are perhaps not that many recorded for them the others have to be played down in order to build Theodoret's heroes up. Whatever the reason, there is a correlation between performing miracles and being known to Theodoret. Indeed, this leads us to conclusions markedly opposite those of Canivet. Theodoret is not sharing our skeptical point of view and including miracles because of the inexorable demands of the genre; rather, he is emphasizing the wonder-working qualities of his family friends.

Chapter 8

Symeon Stylites: A Special Case?

If people know anything about Syrian asceticism or Theodoret's *Religious History* it is normally Symeon of whom they have heard.[1] He is the most famous of the holy men in the work, and it has been argued that his life, number 26, was originally intended to be the last one, the culmination of the work.[2] He lived on a column for forty-five years, and the column rose over fifty feet high, so it is perhaps not surprising that he attracted a lot of attention. He is often the reason why the *Religious History* is referred to or read, and it has been stated that this life is different from the rest, being more conventionally hagiographic in form.[3]

At first sight it might seem as if Symeon's subsequent fame would affect the reading of Theodoret. It is certainly true that Symeon was the holy man on whom later ages focused. A pilgrims' sanctuary grew up around his pillar, and a monastery built there after his death is still visited today.[4] Other ascetics climbed on their pillars in different parts of the empire, even in Trier. Many of the characters in the

---

1. "The Syrians were the 'stars' of the ascetic movement: wild vagrants dressed in skins, their matted hair making them look like eagles, these 'men of fire' amazed and disquieted the Greco-Roman world by their histrionic gestures. Their most typical representatives, in the fifth century, were the 'Stylite' saints — men who squatted on the top of pillars. The founder of this idiosyncrasy, Symeon (ca. 396–459), held court for forty years from the top of a fifty-foot column in the mountainous hinterland of Antioch." (Brown 1971b, 98). See Doran 1992, 16–17, on the different measurements for Symeon's column. Theodoret says 36 cubits (*Religious History* 26.12). See Peeters 1950, 93–136, on Symeon.

2. Devos 1979, 334–35. See also Canivet 1977, 109–12, and Price 1985a, 174, n. 14, on Symeon's fame.

3. Ashbrook Harvey 1988, 378.

4. See Dalrymple 1997, 59–60 on Symeon's monastery today, and 148–49 on a modern stylite.

Religious History are only known about because of Theodoret's writing, whereas we have other lives of Symeon extant.[5] It is clear that Symeon even in his own lifetime was in a league of his own, and this impression is borne out by Theodoret's description of him and his influence.

This life is different from the others in the *Religious History,* and originally it seemed to me that this was because of Symeon's fame. There was less freedom for Theodoret to adapt his material, to personalize it, and he was more constrained to write the story his audience would know. His readers could not but be aware of Symeon since they would already have a substantial body of information about this individual, whereas only the neighboring villagers would have had any acquaintance with an ascetic such as Salamanes. It might seem that Theodoret himself plays a more minor role than one has come to expect. He does in fact turn up in Symeon's life, but at first glance he seems to be playing an uncharacteristically subservient part.

Theodoret begins by stressing Symeon's fame. Other ascetics had received this treatment. We are told that Palladius is famous (πολυθρύλητος, *Religious History* 7.1), that Theodosius is great and famous (μέγας καὶ πολυθρύλητος, 10.1), that everyone knows Macedonius (Μακεδόνιαν . . . ἴσάσι . . . ἅπαντες, 13.1), and that Acepsimas is celebrated throughout the east (οὗ κλέος εὐρὺ κατὰ πᾶσαν τὴν ἕω 15.1), but Symeon is more remarkable than any of these.

> The famous Symeon, the great wonder of the world, is known of by all the subjects of the Roman empire and has also been heard of by the Persians, the Medes, the Ethiopians, and the rapid spread of his fame as far as the nomadic Scythians has taught his love of labor and his philosophy. (26.1)

So people everywhere know of Symeon, inside and outside the empire, Romans and barbarians. Other ascetics in the *Religious History* might be famous, but only Symeon is famous throughout the whole inhabited world. Having given him this fulsome introduction, Theodoret then describes the holy man's early life, but only from the time

5. See Lietzmann 1908, 20–78, for the life of Symeon by Antony; see pages 80–180 for the Syriac life. See Delehaye 1923, 1–17, on the lives of Symeon and the manuscripts, pages 17–24 on other documents that mention him, and pages 24–35 for a survey of the events of his life. For an English translation of the lives of Symeon, see Doran 1992.

of his call to lead a pious life, not from birth. There is a résumé of his early career and his curious dream about digging. He dreamed he was digging foundations, and a voice told him to dig deeper until eventually it said he had dug deep enough and his building would now be effortless. There is also a description of his two years with ascetics, after which he moved to a more formal monastery. From there he was expelled for extreme behavior ten years later.[6] After five days, the superiors of the monastery began to worry and sent two monks to bring him back. To do so they have to pull him out of the cistern where he has decided to live.[7] He spends the next three years in a cottage as a recluse, apparently fed by a local priest, Bassus.

The episode in which Symeon fasts for the first time is rather curious. He tells Bassus not to leave him any food and to seal up his door, the implication being that he was normally fed by this visitor, which gives us an insight into how these ascetics lived. Bassus has to rescue Symeon at the end of his fast, but fortunately the ascetic develops the ability to cope with fasting for a long time. Theodoret remarks that annually for the next twenty-eight years Symeon fasted for forty days (*Religious History* 26.9).[8] At first he was forced to lie down toward the end of his fast; later, when he stood on the pillar, he bound himself in a standing position. Finally, he was able to fast without collapsing or binding himself. Symeon had a tendency to tie himself up because earlier he had tied a harsh cord round his waist so tightly that he bled (26.5), and later we see him tethering himself to a rock with an iron chain so that he cannot leave the area even if he changes his mind. The local bishop, Meletius, points out that if his will were strong enough he would not need to chain himself in this way. Symeon immediately orders a smith to cut off his shackles (26.10).

Symeon displays a certain obstinacy that the church and other monks could see was on the verge of suicidal. Bassus tries to modify his fasting but ultimately is full of admiration for his strength. Theodoret goes on to say that Bassus spreads the story of Symeon's achievement to his own followers (*Religious History* 26.8). Bassus headed a community of like-minded ascetics. It seems relevant that it

---

6. Elliott (1987, 89), discussing the motif of secret flights becoming a topos in saints' lives, contrasts Theodoret's account with that of Antony, who adds the detail that Symeon fled secretly.

7. Elliott (ibid., 105) comments that Symeon came down before going up.

8. This is discussed in Price 1985a, xiv–xv.

is in the story of Symeon, the one clearly disobedient ascetic, that we hear of a monastery with rules laid down for behavior, that of Bassus. Theodoret makes a point of telling us that even though many people have joined this community they do not disobey its rules.

The pillar was, explains Theodoret, an attempt to escape the mass of admirers who thronged around Symeon, trying to touch him or the garments he wore.[9] So even before he had the strange idea of living on a column he was regarded as special. This is how Theodoret wishes to present him to us, although it may seem improbable to us that instead of retreating further into the countryside or desert Symeon had a pillar built for himself, which gradually became taller and taller.[10] Theodoret's elaborate explanation of Symeon's decision to live on a pillar is surely an indication of the incredulity of his readership. He says that the ascetic yearned to be nearer heaven and points out that God has contrived other apparently strange practices, which would astound people and thus draw their attention and make them more likely to listen to the Word of God. So Symeon living on a column is in the same order of things as Isaiah walking naked and barefoot; Jeremiah wearing a loincloth, a wooden collar, and then an iron collar; Hosea taking a harlot for a wife; and Ezekial lying on his right side for 40 days and his left for 150, shaving his head with a sharp sword, and dividing up the shorn hair for various purposes (*Religious History* 26.12).

Theodoret claims that he was an eyewitness to the crowds that gathered round Symeon, crowds so numerous that they almost crushed the author underfoot because Symeon had recommended obtaining a blessing from him. He gives a very vivid description of these admirers, who pulled at his beard as well as his clothing.

I would have been suffocated by their too ardent approach, if he had not used a shout to disperse them. Such is the benefit that the

---

9. Frankfurter (1990) has revived the idea of pagan antecedents for stylitism in Syria, remarking sensibly that for this to have been effective others besides Symeon had to understand something by it. There had to be audience acceptance for Symeon's huge influence to be explicable, that is, he must have been operating in the traditional modes of religious expression in Syria. The famous Lucian passage on which this is based is *De Dea Syria* (28–29). Frankfurter's explanation is rather more probable than Lane Fox's (1997, 216) that "Pillars gave stylites the freedom of choice which we now enjoy from answer-phones."

10. Theodoret is explicit that Symeon ordered a pillar to be built rather than erecting one himself (τιμηθῆναι κελεύσας, *Religious History* 26.12).

pillar mocked by lovers of mockery has poured forth; such is the ray of divine knowledge which it has made descend into the minds of barbarians. (*Religious History* 26.14)

Symeon is portrayed as an extremely influential figure. Even barbarians revered and obeyed him. He was a force to be reckoned with even by secular powers. Symeon's power was extraordinary. It is manifested mostly, though, according to Theodoret, by this influence with vast numbers of people all over the world. He only describes two miracles performed by the ascetic, although he says Symeon performed many. The ascetic cures a paralyzed man, much as Christ did, but, says Theodoret, he performed his miracle through Christ and was not trying to usurp the Master's position (26.16–17). The other miracle was his prayer that the queen of the Ishmaelites would have a child, which she did; that is, she wanted one and asked him to pray for her. Theodoret also describes some of Symeon's successful prophecies. He was clearly a prophet of doom because he foresaw a drought, a crop failure, a famine, and plague, and an attack of locusts. The author ends this list with Symeon's prediction that Theodoret's enemy would die fifteen days before the event actually took place.[11]

There is a cursory account of Symeon's way of life, his humility, and his service to the community by resolving disputes and to the church by fighting pagans, Jews, and heretics. He also roused governors and bishops to greater zeal. Theodoret comments that he has been brief and has tried to give the reader just a taste of the honey. Susan Ashbrook Harvey has said that Theodoret is at his most hagiographic in this life, but it would be difficult to sustain this argument with regard to either content or form.[12] There is an account of his life but only the portion that followed calling, accompanied by a list of the places where he lived. It is not a list of his virtues or his miracles. And he describes Symeon being thrown out of a monastery for being too extreme, thus posing a bad example to others (*Religious History* 26.5). It is also made clear from the story of his first forty-day fast that he would have died had it not been for the ministrations of the local priest, Bassus, who had to revive him. Symeon

---

11. Theodoret does not reveal which enemy this was. The following prophecy about rods from the sky is thought to be an interpolation and is not in most manuscripts.

12. Ashbrook Harvey 1988, 378.

became better at fasting, but without a priest he would have not survived to try. Then it has to be pointed out to him, by the bishop of the area, that there is no need to chain himself to a rock.

So Symeon appears, or Theodoret makes him appear, extreme, obstreperous, and even rather stupid. He fasts almost to death. He persists in practices that make him bleed, which he clearly realizes are disapproved of by the clergy. He fails to realize that chaining himself to a rock is hardly an exercise in willpower. Thus, Theodoret presents Symeon in a less than positive light. Then, when describing his pillar, Theodoret says that people should not criticize but consider the other odd things done by characters in the Bible. In other words, criticism pervades this text. It is true, on the other hand, that Symeon was vulnerable to criticism. In the *Life of Daniel the Stylite,* not by Theodoret, there is a story of monks from Mesopotamia who doubted the virtue of Symeon's procedures and had to repent on meeting the holy man (7–8). But there the criticism is introduced to show how wrong first impressions can be.[13]

The stress is on the power Symeon has over enormous numbers of people, both civilized and not so civilized, at least in the eyes of Theodoret's readers. The potential for trouble is vast, and it would seem possible that this is the intended impression. This particular ascetic was beyond even Theodoret's control, a man who answered only to God, who would defy any authority, ecclesiastical or secular, someone who would act if he saw any wrongdoing.[14]

There are great differences between Theodoret's life of Symeon and those penned by the disciple Antony and the anonymous author of Syriac life, both of whom wrote later.[15] In Antony's version, which

13. The *Life of Daniel the Stylite,* by an anonymous author, is translated by E. Dawes and N. Baynes in *Three Byzantine Saints* (Crestwood, N.Y.: Vladimir's Seminary Press, 1977), 7–84. Theodore Anagnostes (*Ecclesiastical History* 1.12, 2.41) reports that Egyptian monks criticized Symeon. See also the Syriac *Life of Symeon* 117 (translated in Doran 1992, 103–98).

14. Ashbrook Harvey (1998) has written that much of the power of the life of Symeon depends on the liturgical resonances carried by the language and ritual imagery. Her thesis does not work with Theodoret's text, although she uses it as evidence, citing 26.26 to show that Symeon's day is the basic structure of liturgy. Even in the way she describes it, the similarities are less clear than she claims. In any event, one would expect the liturgy to be based on some basic pattern of pious activity. It is simply not true that in Theodoret's account the activities and events of Symeon's vocation culminate in his reception of the Eucharist from Mar Bas (Bassus in the *Religious History*). Interestingly enough, we rarely see holy men in the *Religious History* celebrating Communion.

15. On these two lives, see Flusin 1993, 9.

was written between 459 and 594, Symeon cured a dragon (19) and tied a rope around his body so tightly that his flesh decayed and crawled with worms. He became so putrified that his garments stuck to his rotting body and could not be removed until he was soaked in warm water and oil (5–8). He also threw himself into a well full of evil spirits, snakes, and scorpions (9). In the Syriac life, which is the longest of the three accounts, written between 459 and 474, Symeon develops boils on his left foot, which burst, stink, and swarm with worms. Pus and worms fall to the ground from his foot (48). His miracles are described as better than those of the apostles Peter and Paul (65), and he is even compared to Jesus (108–10).

These texts also differ in their accounts of the aftermath of Symeon's expulsion from the monastery. Antony says that the head of the monastery begged Symeon to tell him what he had learned (11). In the Syriac life, the same character apologizes to Symeon and entrusts the monastery to him on his deathbed (25).[16]

Theodoret's account is thus less flattering to Symeon, and this has been interpreted as being due to his Hellenistic outlook, which was fundamentally unsympathetic to such extreme measures.[17] Both of the other lives have much more vivid, and to the modern reader disgustingly graphic, descriptions of the privations endured by the holy man, and both include the smells endured and enjoyed by those close to him. Ashbrook Harvey argues that this attention to the olfactory is due to a shift in attitudes from Theodoret's day to a more intense physicality in the piety of late antiquity.[18] However, the time difference between the composition of the works is really quite small for such a shift (perhaps twenty years). Theodoret was a classically educated bishop, whereas the authors of the other two lives are purporting at least to be disciples of Symeon, so it would seem that explanations are more likely to be found in the different literary levels of the works. It is not true that Theodoret shows no awareness of the

---

16. Flusin (ibid.) is very interesting on the two works and argues convincingly that the different accounts of the saint's death reflect the difference in the circumstances of composition. The Syriac life was written at Telanissos immediately after Symeon's death and under the control of his disciples, whereas the Greek one was written after he was long dead and reflected the interest in Symeon's body and its translation to Antioch. Lane Fox's judgment is less nuanced. He calls the author of the Greek life, Antony, "a liar" and dismisses the Syriac *Life of Symeon* too (1997, 185, 225).

17. Goehring 1992, 248.

18. Ashbrook Harvey 1999.

sensation of smell, as in chapter 19 of *On Divine Love* it is mentioned explicitly, though only the pleasant version.

If the first edition of the *Religious History* had ended here, or if the original intention was that it should, why did Theodoret carry on?[19] Symeon was the most famous ascetic and already had star quality by the time Theodoret composed his work. The lives that come after Symeon's are those of rather minor characters, Baradatus, Thalelaeus, and the women.[20] All receive only brief notices, and all are very odd: one man lives in a chest, the other in a suspended cage. The women are odd simply by being women. It is unclear what the motivation could have been except to increase the total numbers of lives. Symeon would have been a good individual to end with since he is the most famous of the collection and the only stylite, even though stylitism is a particularly Syrian phenomenon. He is presented as very obstinate and single-minded, a man who inspired and attracted a huge following. The formidable divine approval that he manifested increased his followers. He did not seek power and influence but won them anyway. He was from a poor background, so his achievements are presented as all the more remarkable. He had no social graces and did not need any. He was suffused with divine grace.

---

19. Devos 1979, 334–35.

20. Baradatus was quite prominent by 434, that is, well before Theodoret wrote his work, since he was the recipient of a letter from the Comes Titus along with Jacob of Cyrrhestica, Symeon, and Theodoret himself. See chapter 1 and Schwartz 1936, 23. It seems a little unusual that Theodoret devotes so little space to him, and this may reinforce the theory that these lives were added later rather than being part of the original text.

Chapter 9

Women in the *Religious History*

Given the role women played in the Gospels and the sentiments expressed there about them, subsequent Christian texts were less likely than pagan ones to write women out completely. Given the position of Mary, we are less surprised to read about the mothers of Augustine and Theodoret. It is possible to see why it might have occurred to these writers to introduce them. Cooper and Coon have shown how the introduction of women into Christian discourse probably tells us very little about the real women they purport to describe since their primary role is rhetorical. The following discussion is very much influenced by this assumption.[1]

Because of the paucity of women in non-Christian texts, the females present in works such as the *Religious History* strike the reader. One comes away with the impression that most of the beneficiaries of miracles are women, but in fact this is misleading and there is a fairly equal divide between the sexes.[2] Virtually every other life in the *Religious History* has a female character of some sort in it. Fifteen out of the twenty-eight lives feature at least one woman.[3] Women tend to occur less frequently later in the work. We meet them in ten of the first fourteen lives, whereas out of the last fourteen only five have

---

1. Cooper 1992 and Coon 1997 esp. xi–xxiii, 95–119, 143–47.

2. Life 1 has one woman and four men, life 2 has one woman and six men, life 3 has two women and two men, and in life 6 the recipients are unspecified. Life 7 has one man, life 8 has one woman and three men, life 9 has three women and three men, life 11 has one woman, life 12 has one man, life 13 has three women and three men, life 14 has one man and one woman, life 15 has two men, life 21 has men, life 26 has one queen, and the rest are men or are unspecific.

3. *Religious History* 1, 2, 3, 6, 8, 9, 11, 12, 13, 14, 17, 21, 26, 29, 30 (following Devos 1979 and counting 22 and 23 together and 24 and 25 together).

female characters and two of these are about female ascetics. In Christian texts we expect to meet women portrayed as temptresses or whores, even if reformed, but there is very little discussion of sexual temptation in the *Religious History*.[4] What, one might ask, are women doing in the narrative if they are not tempting men or starving themselves?

Most of the women are described, as one might expect, in terms of their relationship with their families, so we meet children, wives, or mothers. Theodoret usually gives this detail about them but almost never their names. There is one instance in which we are told a woman's name, but it is perhaps significant that, due to a problem in the manuscripts, there is uncertainty about what her name actually was. Possibly it was Astrion, who, we are told with more assurance, was the wife of Ovodianus, a man described as a curial of the highest order (*Religious History* 13.13).[5] She needed help because the diagnosis was that she was either demonically possessed or had a brain disease, the symptoms being that she was delirious and refused to eat or drink. Macedonius cured her.

Macedonius was also called upon to treat the wife of another aristocrat, who suffered from extreme bulimia. Apparently, she ate thirty chickens a day and wanted more. After being cured it seems she retained her taste for the food but was satisfied with only a small piece of chicken a day (*Religious History* 13.9). Another wife, that of Pergamius, the comes orientis, had the same complaint as Theodoret's mother, who was also cured by Peter (9.5). Holy men not only treated eating disorders but helped in matters of love or perhaps sex. The wife of another nobleman went to Aphrahat because her husband was sleeping with another woman, who, she said, had bewitched her husband with magic. Aphrahat, without the aid of spells, somehow canceled those of the rival, allowing the husband to return to his proper bed (8.13).[6]

Perhaps strikingly, and in contrast to works similar to the *Religious History,* women are almost never introduced as the source of sexual temptation for holy men. There is a story in the life of Jacob of Nisibis

4. In Palladius's *Lausiac History* (5) there is a woman who shuts herself away in a tomb because of the effect she has on a man, and in Jerome's *Life of Hilarion* the holy man rebukes a virgin for allowing a demon to possess her (21).

5. See Canivet and Leroy-Molinghen's commentary on this passage (1977–79, 497).

6. This episode is mentioned briefly by Kazhdan (1995, 78).

in which the holy man punishes some girls, by turning their hair gray, for their impudence in staring at him without covering their heads. This episode is unusual both for the sexual undertones — the holy man is clearly disturbed by these young women looking at him — and the rather harsh treatment, although Theodoret comments that at least he did not hand them over to carnivorous bears like Elishah did (*Religious History* 1.5).[7] Elsewhere we see young women being possessed by demons and brought by their parents to holy men for help (3.22, 13.10). There is the rather strange case of a female servant who, being sexually harassed by her master, takes refuge in a convent (9.12–13). The master whips her mother until this unfortunate reveals the hiding place of her daughter. He brings the girl back, but when she flees again he realizes that he cannot win. The story is strange because its moral is unclear. We are not told the fate of the mother, but the daughter develops breast cancer and in her pain calls on the holy man Peter. He eases her agony but does not cure her, and a cynical reader might infer that the message is that one should not be disobedient. One hopes that this was not Theodoret's intention, although it is consistent with the message at the end of *On Divine Love,* where obedience is held up as proof of devotion to God.

Women bringing their children to holy men is one reason why they feature in the narrative, rather as Theodoret's mother had. Theodoret, although he does not give their names, often comments on their social standing, which is predominantly noble (*Religious History* 8.13, 9.5, 13.9, 13.13; see also 3.22 and 14.3). In fact, the only instance in which this is not noted is in the life of Romanus, where Theodoret simply states that this man successfully helped childless women (11.4). Symeon Stylites probably helped other women, but the one Theodoret chooses to tell us about is the queen of the Ishmaelites, who conceived a child after visiting him. Even though she was a monarch, she was not allowed to go near the ascetic and had to send her son to be blessed by him (26.21). The fact that Theodoret comments on social standing would indicate that this was important for some reason. It is possible that it was more significant to help the aristocracy rather than the lowly or that the testimony of the former was worth more than that of the incredulous masses. Noblewomen would perhaps be more interesting to his readers, who would share

---

7. See Krueger 1997b on Theodoret's use of biblical analogies.

their class if not always their gender. Husbands would know where to send their ailing wives.

Perhaps the strangest mother of the *Religious History* is the one who features in the life of Julian Saba (2.17). The holy man was on his way to Antioch to fight heresy when he passed a nobleman's house and the wife begged him to stay with them.[8] He agreed, even though, says Theodoret, he had not seen a woman for forty years. While she was serving him, her seven-year-old son, her only child, fell down a well. When this was reported to her, her curious response was to tell everyone to keep quiet and to put a lid on the aforesaid well, presumably to prevent the noise of the child's screams from disturbing Julian. The latter asked to see her child and persisted when she demurred so that she had to reveal the catastrophe to him. He naturally rescued the poor infant. Theodoret ends the story by saying that this was the reward for the hospitality that the wonderful woman received from the blessed old man.

Women are essential incidental characters because they need the help of holy men, but it is also the case that several holy men do not let women near them. One, Marcianus, is so strict that he will not even see his own sister (*Religious History* 3.14). One wonders what the danger might have been. Other monks were less severe. In one instance, a noblewoman came to the monastery having had a dream that one of their number could help her possessed daughter. The monk who met her told her that the superior did not see women. She was very persistent, and eventually the superior gave in to her tears and presented himself, only to find it was not he who had appeared in her dreams but another disciple of Marcianus, Sabinus (3.21–22). This monk, perhaps unsurprisingly, exorcised her daughter successfully. This is a common feature of holy men. Symeon Stylites, according to Antony's life of him, refused to see his own mother, saying that they would meet in the next life. The poor woman dies without seeing her son and is buried in front of his column (9).

Holy Women

It has been observed that very little can be learned about the real individuals behind the hagiographies of women since one must recog-

---

8. She is compared to Sarah in her hospitality. See Coon 1997, 119, on biblical prototypes for women in hagiography.

nize the rhetorical nature of hagiography and the assumptions on which it is based. The use of women as holy exemplars enables the hope of universal salvation to be emphasized most effectively, for if even women can be saved there is hope for everyone. These texts show us only the views of their authors and not any of the historical reality, or only very little, that may lie behind the texts.[9] It is, though, worth looking at how these women are portrayed to see what the author was trying to say.

The last two lives of the *Religious History* are those of three female ascetics. Theodoret introduces the first, saying:

> For they [women] are worthy of still greater praise, when, despite having a weaker nature, they display the same zeal as the men and free their sex from its ancestral disgrace. (*Religious History* 29.1)

Both of the last two lives are very brief, and at the end of the second Theodoret feels the need to explain again why he has included them. He says that from the beginning of Christianity there have always been female followers of Christ, throughout the empire, who lived by themselves or in communities, choosing a life of self-denial and hymn singing. Earlier in the work, he appeared to be explaining to readers that there are communities of women, as if he thought this might be new to them, but possibly he is just raising the issue (9.12; see also 12.6, where he simply refers to ascetic men and women). He comments that he added accounts of female holiness so that women, too, would have models to follow.[10] One might be tempted to argue that the church needed to hold up models of female sanctity since if women were not allowed near holy men (e.g., 3.14, 3.22, 8.15, 26.21) it would be more difficult for them to learn about them and impossible for them to become followers, as many men did. However, Theodoret says explicitly at the beginning of his life of Domnina that she emulated Maron, who was the male subject of an earlier life (16).

The models Theodoret offered to his female readers were only two in number, and the variations were thus limited. Whereas men could suspend themselves in strange contraptions for years (*Religious History* 28), entomb themselves alive (19), live cramped in a chest that was too small for them (27), perch on a high column (26),

---

9. Ibid., xxi. See also Cameron (1989), who makes a similar point.
10. See Steininger 1997 on the formation of the ideal Christian woman, especially 203–10. See Wilson 1983, 37, on saints being overwhelmingly male.

become a bishop and leader of men (17), or more modestly become a teacher (4), women, on the other hand, could choose only to wear heavy chains and starve themselves or weep continuously and starve themselves (29, 30).[11] Holy women are even more invisible in the *History of the Monks of Egypt,* except that the author mentions communities of women living in Oxyrhynchus (5). Palladius, however, includes far more women in his *Lausiac History* than Theodoret does.[12]

Although many ascetic practices may seem strange to readers today, it is only when describing women that Theodoret mentions madness: "To such a degree has divine yearning driven them to a frenzy, so much has divine love for the Bridegroom driven them mad" (*Religious History* 29.7). But the tone of his account is always one of admiration. He praises women for their suffering, and in essence the only difference between these holy women and their male counterparts is that no man is ever portrayed as weeping, although tears are apparently characteristic of the asceticism of this area.[13] None of the women heal or perform miracles, but these features decline in the work anyway as Theodoret moves on to the living ascetics.[14]

Like the majority of incidental female characters, all three of Theodoret's holy women are noble. In the case of the sisters Marana and Cyra we are told that they despise their family's way of life and chose to live in a small place outside the town (*Religious History* 29). Some of their maidservants wished to share their life so they had another house built for them. This development is similar to those described in connection with followers of male ascetics (e.g., 6.10, 10.3, 22.7) except for the added detail that the sisters had a small window constructed through which they could observe their maidservants and rouse them to prayer (29.2). It is only here that we get any notion of hierarchy or authority being exerted over other ascetics. Indeed, it is the only place where we see servants following their employers into this way of life.

---

11. These are not unusual examples, wealth often being cited in connection with pious women or at least those women men chose to remember. See Cameron 1989, 194–95. Their other activities are usual among female ascetics (Coon 1997, xvii).

12. This is discussed in Elm 1994, 312–14.

13. Vööbus 1960, 283–85.

14. Canivet points out that of the living ascetics only Jacob and Symeon (*Religious History* 21, 26) perform miracles (1977, 119, n. 9). On the various types of miracles, see Kazhdan 1995, 76.

The sisters lived exposed to the elements in an enclosure that had no door, only a window through which food was passed to them. They wore iron weights around their necks, waists, hands, and feet and sheetlike robes that appeared to cover them completely since Theodoret says that they covered their feet, faces, necks, chests, and hands. Given that the clothing must also have enveloped their legs, torsos, and arms, it would seem that nothing of their bodies was visible. Usually they received no company except at Whitsuntide, when they spoke to female visitors; again the segregation of the sexes, which was unusual enough for us to hear about it, necessitated the existence of female ascetics if women were to participate in asceticism. Marana spoke to visitors through the window. Theodoret comments that no one had ever heard Cyra utter a word. She was less robust than her sister and was permanently bent over from the heavy weights she carried. Theodoret specified that Marana spoke to women who came to visit. There is no mention of male visitors except for himself. He informs us that he had often been inside their enclosure since they told him to dig through the door, which was normally walled up with clay and stones. He says that they wished to see him out of respect for his episcopal office. He thus had seen the heavy weights they carried and persuaded them to take them off but adds that they donned them again once he left (*Religious History* 29.5).

This couple is unusual in that they are siblings living together, there being no similar case among the male ascetics Theodoret describes. The last woman he mentions is also different in that her isolation or withdrawal from the world is far less dramatic than that of her male counterparts. Domnina chooses to live at the bottom of her mother's garden (*Religious History* 30.1). She, like the previous two women, eats very little, although she provides others with food and provisions. Again this is different from the men, who are fed by others. She is able to do this, Theodoret tells us, because she has the property of her mother and brothers at her disposal (30.3). Theodoret gives us a vivid description of her emaciation. She is skeletally thin, fat and muscle having been worn away by physical labor, and her skin is like a film over her bones. He adds, however, that she wears a voluminous cloak, which swathes her, even her head, so that she literally sees no one and in turn no one sees her face. Theodoret may be placing this emphasis on the all-embracing clothes that the female ascetics wear (in other words, their extreme modesty) because they presumably never allowed males other than the bishop to approach them. Theodoret describes Domnina as bent to her knees as if she were permanently in this position. She always spoke, amid her tears, softly and indistinctly (λεπτὰ δὲ λίαν καὶ ἄσημα φθεγγομένη). The word ἄσημος can also mean inarticulately or meaninglessly, but one would presume that Theodoret is not being insulting here (30.2).

He says that Domnina often took his hand, placed it on her eyes, and released it soaked with tears. Theodoret's next sentence is: "What discourse could give due praise to a woman who with such wealth of philosophy weeps and wails and sighs like those living in extreme poverty?" (*Religious History* 30.2). Several things are interesting here. First, Theodoret uses contrast for effect with his terms *wealth of philosophy* and *extreme poverty.* Then there is the admission that this woman is not actually poor. She is still living in her mother's garden and uses her family wealth to finance her charity. Finally, we learn that a woman who cries all the time cannot be praised enough. Weeping was an important aspect of Syrian asceticism, along with fasting and praying. Ephraim commented that laughter is to be understood as an unmistakable symptom that evil has entered the soul and is working to destroy the blessedness of salvation promised only to those who are sad.[15] Given such an attitude toward tears, it is tempting to see this episode as an example of Theodoret's Hellenization of his Syrian world. That is, to make his characters more acceptable to his Greek audience he adapts his material slightly. One might say that Greek literature has a tradition of crying men from Achilles onward, but it does not seem to be a feature of the Roman world.[16] Tears do occur in the *Religious History,* but they are only shed by women. The second half of the life of Domnina is taken up with general reflections on female ascetics and then on Theodoret's task as a whole.

The two narratives of women are very short and appear to have been added as an afterthought. As the material is so scant, one cannot generalize adequately, but it can be observed that the women are not leaders of communities in the same way their male counterparts are since their followers are maidservants to whom they still

---

15. Vööbus 1960, 282–85.
16. Walbank 1967, 96, on Polybius 8.20, comments that Antiochus crying at the fate of Achaeus was the mark of the sensibility of a Hellenistic prince.

give orders of a sort. The women are wealthy and retain their wealth in order to maintain themselves, whereas we read of men giving their property up (e.g., in 5.1 and 12.7). They do not leave their homes, as the men frequently do (e.g., in 3.1, 8.1, and 9.1–3). Women cry and perform no miracles. They are impressive, it would seem, merely because they are female and live under rather harsh conditions. The role of women in the *Religious History* appears to conform to the theory that women are included in hagiographic texts to allow for the possibility of universal salvation.[17] If even women can be saved, there is hope for everyone.

However, to give Theodoret his due, he does at least include women. These women, few though they are, are presented as admirable and described in glowing terms. The difference between the sexes is quantative rather than qualitative in that women are simply weaker than men. Theodoret's reference to ancestral disgrace is hardly unusual and indeed is rather restrained for some Christian authors (*Religious History* 29.1). Although he may have only added female ascetics as an afterthought, women occur throughout the *Religious History* and not, as a cynical modern reader might expect, as temptations for holy men to overcome. Indeed, there is virtually nothing of this in the work. It is worth remembering that in the *Cure for Hellenic Maladies* he puts forward some very enlightened views, saying that men and women differ only in their bodies, not their souls, and that women have the same powers of reason as men. Sometimes they judge what should be done better than men and can offer good advice (5.57). The die-hard conservative would note that in the same book he also says that barbarians are as good as Greeks.

From an examination of his extremely short accounts of holy women, it would seem reasonable to assert that Theodoret is not really interested in this phenomenon. In *On Divine Love* his assumption is that the ascetics are male when he argues that they face much greater hardships than sailors or workers because they do not have wives to look after them (3). His focus was on holy men, and he was concerned to portray them as being not only on his side in any theological struggle but very much under his influence, perhaps even under his control, if this term is not too loaded.

---

17. Coon 1997, xxi. See also Cameron 1989 on the problems of understanding early Christian texts adequately. As she argues, texts that purport to be about women are often more concerned with theology.

Christian texts were concerned to include women. From its earliest beginnings, Christianity had displayed a revolutionary interest in the dispossessed. Subsequent writers could not ignore this powerful tradition, even though they may have been educated in the pagan classics, which generally had no place for the female sex except as a negative contrast to the male. Theodoret shows the tension between the two traditions by allowing women a place in his narrative but keeping their heroics to a minimum. This is not the full story, however, as will be discussed in the next chapter.

PART III

Interaction with Clerics

Chapter 10

The Relationship between the Ascetics and the Church

Having looked at who the subjects of the *Religious History* were, where they came from, what language they spoke, how they lived, what they did, and what role women play in the text, it is necessary to examine the relationship between these characters and the church. It has often been remarked that the growth of monasticism was a reaction to the growing acceptance of Christianity in society as a whole, and that in some sense it posed an enormous threat to the established church, one that the church skillfully tamed, or perhaps harnessed, for its own ends. Men of the church appear in the *Religious History,* and there is an unmistakable deference shown to them on the whole. However, there are also passages such as the following.

> Then, taking his stick (because of old age he was wont to walk with support), he [Macedonius] pursued the bishop himself and all those present, for he supposed that the ordination would deprive him of the mountaintop and the life he loved. (*Religious History* 13.4)

Macedonius was a fearless individual. In chapter 5 we saw him reproaching the emperor; here he is chasing a bishop (Flavian, bishop of Antioch in this case) with a stick. It is not by chance that this particular holy man is very closely associated with Theodoret's family. However, here it is the relationship with the bishop that I wish to examine. The episode just cited, paradoxically, demonstrates respect for the church and its offices rather than the opposite, in contrast to first impressions. In fact, what we see in the *Religious History* is a very strong message that the correct and desirable relationship between holy man and cleric is deference from the former and leadership from the latter. We can also see throughout the text that in Theodoret's view it is more difficult to be a priest (and more difficult still to be a bishop) than it is to be a holy man. Theodoret appears several times in the text in his capacity as bishop, and the encounters all demonstrate in the clearest possible manner that bishops, particularly Theodoret, are natural leaders and guides for these zealous and remarkable but otherworldly and thus naive ascetics.

It is a common feature of hagiography that the subjects of the lives are shown as obedient and deferential to men of the cloth. Cynics might argue that this, rather than the celebration of the individual saint, is the real purpose behind it.[1] It is undeniable, and indeed has been remarked upon before, that this trait occurs fairly noticeably in the *Religious History*. Canivet ends his book by drawing attention to this aspect.

> La respectueuse obéissance des moines à l'épiscopat va évidemment a l'Eglise. Theodoret y insiste encore en vantant leur fidélité à "la discipline ecclésiastique" et leur dévouement à la cause de l'orthodoxie, toutes manifestations de l'amour de Dieu qui, précisement, leur fera accepter, le cas échéant, la charge de pasteur.[2]

The obedience of monks was a preoccupation for the church in the first half of the fifth century, as can be seen simply by looking at the canons that resulted from the Council of Chalcedon, which lay down regulations for their control. Sometimes monks become priests or bishops themselves, and as Theodoret himself falls into this group it is useful to see how he views himself or at least how he wishes others to view him.[3]

---

1. See, for example, Van Dam 1993, 69–81, on Gregory of Tours's cultivation of Martin, which is described by Fouracre (1999, 147) thus: "Gregory was, as Van Dam has argued, hanging onto his job by the hem of Martin's cloak."

2. Canivet 1977, 290. Cf. Brakke's analysis of the relationship between Athanasius and local monks (1995, 81–82).

3. Philip Rousseau has written perceptively on the nature of the *Religious History*, and this chapter is a development of some of his views (1997). See also Rousseau 1978, 56–67, on ascetics in the church and pages 148 and 164 on Martin's position as bishop and the importance of this for Sulpicius Severus. See Rousseau 1971 on the use of hagiographic literature in the service of the church.

One of the most famous members of the church to appear in the *Religious History* is Bassus. He is well known because he appears in the life of the most celebrated ascetic of them all, Symeon Stylites. Bassus supervised local priests and apparently visited and fed holy men like Symeon.[4] As we have seen, Symeon asked him not to leave any food for forty days, as he wished to fast. Bassus advocates a more moderate approach, pointing out that suicide is not a virtue, so they compromise: Bassus leaves the food, which Symeon can ignore if he wishes. Bassus returns after forty days and finds Symeon unable to move or speak, not having touched the food. Bassus revives him and goes back to his own followers and tells them of this marvel.

Bassus is interesting in that, although he is clearly a part of the church hierarchy, he is also the head of a community of ascetics, who, unusually in Theodoret's account, have rules by which they must live. They are not allowed to possess horses or mules, accept gifts of money, or pass through the gate of the monastery to buy something or see a friend (*Religious History* 26.8). We do not see many priests as heads of communities. The priest in this life is actually of crucial importance to Symeon, who presumably would have died had Bassus not checked on him at the end of forty days. A local priest plays a similarly supportive role in the life of Domnina, who sends her visitors to stay with him (30.3).

In the life of Polychronios, Theodoret describes how a great number of priests came to this holy man during a drought. One asked if he would stretch his hand over a flask, but he refused (*Religious History* 24.7). The priest then stood behind the ascetic while he prayed and held out his flask, which filled with oil. Others held out their hands and found they had oil in them. Here we see priests showing faith that the holy man can help them and insisting on receiving his help whether he wants to give it or not. The holy man is virtually passive here. His negative answer is not even given by himself. Theodoret simply reports that the priest who asked was told by another that the ascetic would not comply. The priest is active here,

---

4. Theodoret calls Bassus a supervisor of local priests (πολλὰς περιώδευε κώμας τοῖς κατὰ κώμην ἱερεῦσιν ἐπιστατῶν, 26.7), which is a periphrasis for the duties of a periodeutes or itinerant priest (Canivet and Leroy-Molinghen 1977–79, 173, n. 2). See also Escolan 1999, 329–31, on "periodeutes" and "chorepiscopi." On these terms, see also H. Leclerq in Cabrol 1907 and "chorepiscopus" in Livingstone 1997. Theodoret refers to presbyters who are chorepiscopi as well as Alypius, the exarch of the monks, in letters 113, 116, and 17.

and his faith is rewarded. The holy man is presented as almost literally a fountain of divinity that others can tap into if they wish, and if they know how.

In the *Religious History,* there are several holy men who are also priests. For instance, there is Abraham, who was begged by his local village to be its priest. He agrees but three years later hands over his duties to one of his companions and goes back to his monastery (17.4).[5] The first time we read about an ordination of a monk in the *Religious History* it is a failure. Some bishops came to try to ordain Marcianus, but none dared to do so and they left without having achieved their purpose (3.11). In the life of Eusebius of Teleda we learn that Olympius, one of his companions, was a priest ("honored with the priesthood," says Theodoret). He is a rather curious figure since he is used as an example of bad behavior. Olympius rails against Eusebius,

> calling his forbearance a general injury, saying that his gentleness was harmful to everyone and calling his consummate philosophy not forbearance but folly. (4.10)

Theodoret adds that he was Roman by race (τὸ μὲν γένος ʽΡωμαῖος). This is an interesting detail, and presumably by this Theodoret means that the man was a westerner. One wonders if he is trying to explain his manners because the man is only introduced to insult the ascetic and reveal the latter's remarkable tolerance. Whatever the reason, this is an example of a priest living in a community but in a position of influence since he was second in authority, similar in some ways to Bassus perhaps.

One of the subjects of a life, the first one from Cyrrhus, Maësymas, was a priest, "having been conspicuous in the solitary life" (*Religious History* 14.2). After spending time as a monk he was ordained and placed in charge of a village, which Theodoret seems to feel might exclude him from his category of holy men except that he continued to live an ascetic life. He ends his account as follows.

> One can learn from them that those who choose to practice philosophy are harmed not at all by life in towns and villages; for this

---

5. See Chitty 1966, 31–32, 53–54, 85; and Escolan 1999, 267–311, on monks becoming priests and bishops.

man and those like him responsible for the service of God have shown that it is possible even for those who go about among many to attain the very summit of the virtues. (14.5)

Theodoret seems to be arguing that priests are at least the equals of holy men. He is saying that it is harder to live virtuously in society, by which he means normal communities like villages rather than ascetic communities, than outside it. This is borne out by other comments in the work. At the beginning of the fourth life, that of Eusebius of Teleda, he comments that he will now write about holy men who live in the inhabited land (as opposed to residing in the desert, as the first three ascetics did) and show that even here people can achieve virtue (4.1). Later in this life he describes how Eusebius was persuaded to leave his isolation by the arguments of another ascetic, Ammianus, who chided him for self-love and pressed the case for saving other souls as well as his own (4.4). Similarly, when talking about Asclepius (25.1), he says that this ascetic was able to live in a village ("mixing with the multitude" seems rather an exaggerated way of describing village life, but this is Theodoret's phrase) without harm. Theodoret even says that because of this he will receive a double crown. Clearly, it is more spectacular to live virtuously in society than outside it, which is perhaps a little unexpected to a naive reader expecting to read a eulogy of holy men.

Being a priest was difficult because it entailed living in society. To return to the episode mentioned at the beginning of this chapter, after Macedonius was tricked into coming to Antioch so that Flavian, the bishop, could ordain him he was so angry that he chased the offending bishop with a stick, "for he supposed that the ordination would deprive him of the mountaintop and the life he loved" (*Religious History* 13.4). He was so upset by the duplicity that he refused to come to the city again until some friends told him he could not be ordained twice. Theodoret tells the reader what was in Macedonius's mind. He thought he was losing the way of life he loved. In other words, Theodoret is interpreting his refusal as a form of selfishness. The man is refusing to sacrifice his way of life to serve the church, whereas one might have thought that ascetics wished to sacrifice things they loved to prove their devotion to God. Ordination in fact did not make any difference to Macedonius's life, but it was the assumption that it would do so that horrified him rather than anything intrinsic in the ordination. Given that he did not have to perform any priestly duties, it is interesting that Flavian was so keen for him to be ordained.[6] And we see this elsewhere.

The life of Acepsimas is short, and the following episode makes up a large proportion of it. When this ascetic learned that he was terminally ill he received all visitors. The bishop pressed him to be ordained, and eventually the holy man agreed, saying,

> Since I am emigrating from here in a few days, I shall not quarrel about this. If I were going to live for a long time, I would utterly have fled from the heavy and fearful burden of the priesthood, terrified at answering for the deposit. But since in no long time I shall depart and leave what is here, I shall accept obediently what you command.[7] (*Religious History* 15.4)

In other words, it is easier to starve oneself for days, live out in the freezing cold and blazing heat, wear chains, and generally live without ordinary human comforts for years than to be a priest. These words are uttered by an ascetic, but we should perhaps remember that it is Theodoret who put them in his mouth. The trials of the priesthood have been well documented by priests such as John Chrysostom, who wrote a whole treatise on it, *On the Priesthood*.[8] In the sixth book he makes the same comparison and says that it is more difficult to be a priest than a holy man because a holy man has only his own soul to look after while the priest has responsibility for those of his whole flock (6.3).[9]

---

6. There was a difference between an honorary priesthood and a priesthood with pastoral responsibilities. Some sought ordination in order to avoid their curial duties, which was why Canon 6 of the Council of Chalcedon forbade absolute ordination, that is, ordination that did not involve a specific pastoral charge. I owe this observation to Richard Price.

7. After this passages comes a comment about the holy man being like a bride, which is discussed in chapter 12. Cassian thought that monks should not want to be priests but also that they should not refuse the office (*Conferences* 4.11), on which see Rousseau 1978, 217. See pages 125–32 on Jerome and the priesthood.

8. This work may be more about the episcopate than the priesthood proper, since the purported occasion of its composition is the elevation of the author and his friend Basil to the rank of bishop, but his remarks are very general. My thanks go to Richard Price for drawing my attention to this.

9. For a discussion of this and similar comments by other writers, see Dudley 1991. Leadership was not only burdensome; it could be dangerous. Benedict was begged by monks to be their abbot, but he was so strict that they regretted it and tried to poison

The church was very keen to incorporate these men into its hierarchy. The episode with Acepsimas stresses the notion of obedience, and priests had to obey their bishops, or at least that's what they were supposed to do. Perhaps the oddest character in the work, Salamanes, is also ordained. He is odd because he seems to be comatose. He makes no response to being ordained nor to any other event that befalls him such as being carried off to another village and then reclaimed by his original village. He is completely passive, living in a cell with no door or window, and he does not seem to move or speak at all. He performs no miracles but is seen as holy and a desirable presence in one's community (*Religious History* 19.3). Given his inaction, it is surely interesting that the bishop wished to ordain him (19.2). Theodoret praises him for being totally dead to this life (οὕτω νεκρὸν ἑαυτὸν παντελῶς τῷ βίῳ κατέστησε, 19.3). Theodoret says that the bishop came because he had learned of Salamanes' virtue and wanted to give him the gift of the priesthood. As we have seen in the previous cases, some holy men, at least those described by Theodoret, saw the priesthood more as a burden than a gift, but one must suppose that it was an honor to be deemed worthy of such high office.[10]

Some monks are burdened not only with the priesthood but with episcopal rank.[11] There are Acacius of Beroea, for whom Theodoret reserves very elevated praise (see, e.g., *Religious History* 2.9; he is also mentioned in *Ecclesiastical History* 5.4), Agapetus of Apamea (3.5; see also in *Ecclesiastical History* 5.27), Aphthonius (5.8), and Helladius of Cilicia (10.9).[12] Of Acacius Theodoret says:

> I mean the famous, the celebrated one, preeminent in the monastic life, who emitted bright beams of virtue and was counted worthy of the episcopal office and assigned to be shepherd of Beroea. (*Religious History* 2.9)

---

him (Gregory the Great's *Life of Benedict* 3.2–4). He was a rather unfortunate individual, as later on a priest also tried this (8.2). Athanasius told Dracontius that before he was made bishop, he (Dracontius) had lived for himself but afterward he lived for his flock (*Epistle* 49).

10. This resembles the leaders in Plato's *Republic,* perhaps; see, for example, 7.520d.

11. See Canivet 1969, 230–33, on the way Theodoret refers to the rank of bishop.

12. See Canivet 1977, 27–29, on the relationship between the *Ecclesiastical History* and the *Religious History.*

He describes Agapetus in this way.

> The great Agapetus, when he had received the necessary training and exercise and learnt well this athletic skill departed, as I said, and sowed the seeds he had received from that godly soul. He became so notable and celebrated that he was counted worthy of an episcopal see. (3.5)

What we are seeing here is a progression. Agapetus, trained and having perfected his skill, went on to use it. He "became *so* notable and celebrated *that*" (my emphasis) he became a bishop (οὕτω δὲ περιφανὴς ἐγένετο καὶ περίβλεπτος ὡς). There is no ambivalence here. In terms of hierarchy, the rank of bishop was the top. However remarkable these holy men were, being a bishop was something for which only the very best were considered. It was an honor only a few could attain. Two of these wonders were the subjects of lives: Jacob of Nisibis, whose story is the first in the work; and Abraham (17).

Jacob of Nisibis is one of the few people in the *Religious History* for whom we have other records.[13] He holds a key position in the *Religious History,* his being the first life to be recounted, a position Theodoret comments on later in the text (21.2). Jacob is an interesting figure with which to begin the work since he had a career similar to Theodoret's own; both had been in a monastic community before reluctantly accepting the post of bishop.[14] Theodoret begins the life by comparing his own task with that of Moses, saying that like his famous predecessor he needed the help of the Holy Spirit in his work. Jacob is compared favorably with Old and New Testament figures, including Moses (1.5, 1.11).[15]

Again we encounter the notion that being appointed bishop is reserved only for those preeminent in merit. After recounting a couple of miracles that Jacob performed, Theodoret says:

---

13. Canivet and Leroy-Molinghen 1977–79, 60–63; Drijvers 1981.

14. Bundy 1991. Peeters (1920) conducts a careful examination of all the sources on Jacob.

15. See Krueger 1997b, esp. 409–11, on the typological figuration in this life. Moses is often used (see Rapp 1998). See Van Uytfanghe 1993, esp. 172–77, on typology used in hagiography.

Because he was conspicuous for these actions and beloved by all and his name circulated in everyone's mouth, he was compelled to accept the office of bishop. (*Religious History* 1.7)

Despite his elevation, Jacob maintained his ascetic way of life, and his new post made his life more arduous since he had such extra duties as caring for widows and orphans and deciding cases of wrong-doing. Perhaps Theodoret is suggesting that bishops should be chosen from among the ascetics since ascetic spirituality provides the social and religious power that the church needs to fight its enemies: heretics or demonic powers or simply unsympathetic secular ones.[16] The passage quoted in the previous paragraph seems to disprove, or at least cast doubt on, this thesis since Theodoret is surely expressing surprise at the fact that Jacob does not abandon his asceticism. Indeed, he comments on the same point in the life of Abraham, that is, that even though he was made a bishop he still lives ascetically, as if this were the exception rather than the rule. This is why he has included him in his *Religious History* (17.11).

Theodoret introduces Abraham with what is almost an apology (or at least an explanation). He says that although he was a bishop he will include him because of his great worth (17.1). In other words, it would seem that the fact that he was a bishop might otherwise have excluded him from the work. In any case, only these two holy men, Jacob and Abraham, are also bishops, so it does not seem likely that the appointment of bishops from the body of monks was high on Theodoret's agenda. One should also note, however, that Theodoret tells us that Abraham was a native of the Cyrrhus region (17.1). The readers learns that Cyrrhus had produced at least one saintly bishop, although that was not Abraham's see.

When Abraham converts a village by lending the villagers money to pay their taxes they beg him to become their patron (προστάτης, *Religious History* 17.3), as if they had all read Peter Brown.[17] (Abraham had borrowed a hundred gold pieces from friends to lend to the villagers, as discussed in chapter 5.) He agrees to be their patron if they promise to build a church, which they do immediately. He then

---

16. This was suggested by Bundy (1991, 244).

17. See Browning 1981, 127: "It is almost as if the hagiographers had read Lévi-Strauss." On the holy man as patron see Brown 1971a.

tells them to appoint a priest, and they beg him to take the post. After a while, however, he gives this up and returns to his monastery (17.4). Later "after gaining fame," as if this is somehow relevant (compare the similar circumstances of Jacob's elevation [1.7], and this is also a factor in the cases of Acacius and Agapetus [2.9, 3.5]), he is made bishop of Carrhae and clears this city of heresy. This is perhaps an important function of a bishop, since Jacob of Nisibis is famous for his opposition to Arius (1.10), and Theodoret himself took pride in ridding his diocese of such filth, as he tells the bishop of Rome (*Epistle* 113). After describing such activities such as greeting guests and judging lawsuits, Theodoret mentions that even the emperor wanted to see Abraham, a man who did not even speak Greek (17.9).[18] Upon his death he was given a big funeral and his body was taken to Antioch, where officials had to protect it from relic hunters.

Theodoret is not alone in presenting the clergy in this very positive light. It is interesting to consider how many saints' lives portray their subjects as either playing a supportive role to their clergy, such as Antony helping in the struggle against the Arians (*Life of Antony* 69), or being men of the church themselves.[19] Martin of Tours is an obvious example since he is described as a good bishop, as opposed to the evil ones who criticized him (Sulpicius Severus *Life of Martin of Tours* 27.3).[20] Theodore of Sykeon was made a priest at eighteen and was then promoted to bishop (*Life of Theodore of Sykeon* 23). John the Almsgiver was made a bishop without this intermediary stage (*Life of John the Almsgiver* 4).[21] In other words, the church was creating a genre that glorified itself while appearing to eulogize individuals or, as Rousseau expresses it in relation to Sulpicius Severus, sanctity was being harnessed to the purposes of the church. An influential pattern of admiration, discipleship, and obedience was being set up for the next generation of churchmen.[22]

This is not the full story, however. There is one bishop who

---

18. See Urbainczyk 2000.

19. Brakke (1995, 110) argues that in the *Life of Antony* (chapter 67) Athanasius illustrates the ideal relationship between monk and bishop.

20. This is discussed by Rousseau (1978, 143–51), who observes that probably the most important thing about Martin is that he was a bishop (148).

21. He was of noble birth and already had a family (having been forced by his father-in-law to have sex with his wife). Fortunately for him, his wife and all his sons died (*Life of John the Almsgiver* 3).

22. Rousseau 1978, 165.

appears regularly throughout the *Religious History* in no fewer than ten lives, that is, Theodoret himself (18, 20, 21, 22, 24, 25, 26, 28, 29, 30). The life of Jacob of Cyrrhestica is the longest in the whole *Religious History,* and it is also the one in which Theodoret plays the largest role (21).[23] Possibly because Theodoret is claiming first-hand knowledge of his subject, we learn much more about the struggles of the holy man in this life than in any other. Theodoret achieves this by allotting him fairly sustained passages of direct speech. In this respect, the life of Jacob is nearer the tradition of the *Life of Antony* than are the other lives in the work. Theodoret's role here reveals his unequivocal view of the relationship between himself, and possibly bishops in general, and the holy men about whom he was writing.

Out of the five main episodes in which Theodoret appears, four represent him as rescuing Jacob in some way. In the first, he describes the ascetic's extreme practices, which include never seeking refuge from the gaze of onlookers even when sick. On this Theodoret comments, memorably, "Nor are other men who have had a respectable upbringing ready to evacuate excrement in the presence of strangers" (*Religious History* 21.5). This perhaps tells us more about the behavior of badly brought up late antique citizens than we might wish to know. Theodoret gets rid of Jacob's audience using, he says, his episcopal authority (τὰ τῆς ἱεροσύτης αὐτοῖς δεσμὰ περιτέθηκα) and the next day persuades the holy man to sit in the shade, rather than the blazing sun, by claiming to have a headache himself (21.6). In the next paragraph he tricks Jacob into lying down and in the next persuades him with words of enchantment to remove his iron weights. Jacob falls even more ill, but this time Theodoret is away and the holy man falls prey to the pious, who come to seize him. Word is sent to Theodoret, who rushes back to find Jacob unconscious. The holy man opens his eyes at the sound of Theodoret's voice and asks to be taken back to the mountain, which Theodoret arranges immediately. This little drama illustrates two themes that recur throughout the whole work. One is that sometimes these paragons of virtue have to be rescued from themselves (see, e.g., 24.4, 6, and 29.5).[24] The other, which is related, is the crucial, sometimes lifesaving role played by the church in the lives of

---

23. It is thirty-five chapters long. The chapter on Symeon is twenty-eight.

24. See Gribomont's comments on Theodoret's views of asceticism (1981, 46).

these ascetics (21.7). When Jacob asks to return home, it is Theodoret who sees that his wishes are carried out.

The next episode is introduced by Theodoret as a demonstration
of how he was helped by Jacob. This is the episode in which a demon
speaks to Theodoret in Syriac, telling him that he is protected by
Jacob (*Religious History* 21.15).[25] The notion of the ascetic helping
the bishop might seem rather uncharacteristic, except that we do see
holy men coming to help in struggles against heresy, as noted earlier.
It should also be noted that this incident reflects very well on Theodoret, who we now learn is struggling heroically against Marcionites,
clearly with God on his side. The aid Theodoret receives from the
holy man is merely confirmation that he is on the side of truth. And,
although Theodoret says he is assisted by Jacob, it emerges that he
has better knowledge of divine matters than the holy man does.
Theodoret had always known that the relics he received from Palestine were those of John the Baptist. Jacob was more skeptical and
had to receive a vision from John himself, who reprimanded him for
his doubts (21.20).

Theodoret relates Jacob's experiences with demons, which he had
confided to the bishop before narrating the story of his tomb. Some
people had built a shrine for Jacob in the village whereas Theodoret
had prepared a place in the Shrine of the Apostles (*Religious History*
21.30). Jacob, on the other hand, asked to be buried on the mountain
where he had lived. Theodoret agrees and makes arrangements for
this. At first, one might think that here we see the holy man overrid-
ing an episcopal decision, or at least a disagreement of some kind,
but one can also see this as Theodoret wishing to honor the modest
ascetic. Being the recipient of Jacob's statements about his own desires, he makes sure that they are carried out. In other words, he is
necessary to the holy man for the execution of his wishes. Jacob may
know what he wants, but the bishop is the man with the power to
make the practical arrangements. Similarly, when Jacob was thought
to be dying Theodoret ensures that he is returned to the mountain, as
he requests (21.10).

At this stage it would seem that there is not much more for
Theodoret to say about Jacob. The life contains the feats of endur-

---

25. See chapter 5. It is a feature of saints that they struggle with demons. This is
hardly a struggle, but it shows that Theodoret is on the right side and in the right tradition.
See Browning 1981, 122.

ance performed by him, conquering hunger, cold, and demons, and it also describes his miracles. In the chapter following the discussion of where he will be buried, Theodoret calls Jacob a great man as if drawing the narrative to a close (*Religious History* 21.31). Before finishing, however, he raises the issue of criticism of Jacob. Some, he says, have called Jacob bad tempered. He has asked the ascetic about his behavior and purports to give Jacob's response to this charge. Unusually, three chapters are devoted to dealing with the censure of, or at least disapproving remarks about, an ascetic; the only other place where this occurs, though more briefly, is in the life of Symeon (26.12). Of course, in both cases Theodoret is responding to criticism, but it is still interesting that he brings the matter up. He ends the longest life with the comment that he has been brief and that his account was narrative not panegyric. As Rousseau points out, this is a bishop's account and the criticism is part of that.[26] Not only does the holy man have to be protected from his own asceticism, but his almost fanatical devotion to God makes him vulnerable to unpopularity among the ordinary people, those who come to him for help or out of piety. The bishop is needed to protect the ascetic from himself and to mediate between him and the laity. This is a remarkable twist to the situation, as it is sometimes perceived, in which the holy man is an intermediary for the ordinary and the divine.[27] Theodoret turns this around to make the holy man inaccessible and the bishop the go-between. Without Theodoret, Jacob would have been bullied, vilified, and dead as well as forgotten.[28]

This life places Theodoret at center stage in the work. He is a bishop who enjoys a very special, indeed unique, relationship with the marvel that is Jacob. This exceptional bond with ascetics can be seen in other lives, where he is shown extraordinary respect by them. Eusebius of Asikha permitted only few people to enter his cell but allowed Theodoret in. And although he refused to speak to anyone else he talked with Theodoret and kept him for a long time, discoursing on matters of heaven (*Religious History* 18.2). Maris often welcomed Theodoret and discussed philosophy with him, claiming that he had never experienced such delight as receiving Communion from him (20.4). Limnaeus refused any visitors but Theodoret, so that

26. Rousseau 1997, 38.
27. This is noted in Brown 1971a and taken up energetically in Rapp 1999.
28. Without Bassus, Symeon would have died.

anyone who wished to see him rushed round when they learned he was coming in the hope of entering with him (22.3). Jacob of Nimouza sees no one but digs through the door himself, although he is more than ninety years old, in order to welcome Theodoret into his cell (25.2). Symeon tells his admirers that they will benefit from Theodoret's blessing, which must have been rather gratifying for the bishop (26.14), and Domnina, a woman who eats only soaked lentils and whose body is worn to skin and bone, sends not just lentils but rolls and fruit for Theodoret's consumption (30.3) Theodoret is telling us in all these cases that he is honored in a very singular way by these holy individuals. They treat him as they treat no others. They clearly recognize his worth.

One reaction to this might be to assume that this is the way holy men treat all bishops. Although Theodoret emerges from his encounters with his subjects very well, this is not true of all bishops.[29] In the life of Marcianus, as mentioned earlier, Flavian of Antioch and other bishops, unable to pluck up the courage to ordain the holy man, leave frustrated in their wish. The unfortunate Flavian also appears in the passage at the beginning of this chapter (*Religious History* 13.4). This rather strange episode is clarified a little later when we learn that Macedonius only spoke Syriac, which is why he had not realized what was happening to him (13.7). Theodoret says he is narrating the story to show how simple Macedonius was. It seems that he generally wishes to portray his holy men as simple, so simple that they need less simple people like himself to help them.[30]

Flavian, then, is an example of a rather unsuccessful bishop. Elsewhere there are more positive representations. In the life of Zeno, that ascetic entrusts all his worldly possessions to the bishop Alexander of Antioch, "since you are a bishop and live a life worthy of the episcopal office," the implication surely being that not all incumbents are. Theodoret does not tell us here but he does in the *Ecclesiastical History* that Alexander had been a monk before being made bishop (5.35.1–2).[31] Other passages in which bishops appear in the

---

29. See Canivet 1977, 289–90, on how Theodoret shows the monks obeying the bishops.

30. Heliodorus, for example, was so removed from ordinary life, having been in the monastery since he was three, that he claimed not to know what pigs or cocks or other such animals looked like (*Religious History* 26.4).

31. The information comes in the middle of the story of John Chrysostom, another ascetic who became a bishop.

texts occur when they come to ordain ascetics (*Religious History* 15.4, 19.2). It is perhaps worth noting that we never see Theodoret doing this. An episode that more closely resembles those featuring Theodoret, occurs in the life of Symeon where Meletius, the bishop of Antioch at the time, remarks to the future stylite that he need not chain himself to a rock. Symeon took this to heart and asked a smith to remove his irons (26.10). In the following life, Baradatus shuts himself up in a tiny wooden chest but is persuaded to leave it by another bishop of Antioch, Theodotus (27.3).

Bishops do receive honor, and Theodoret receives more than others. There are two issues here. One is that Theodoret does seem to hold the view, which might appear antithetical to the lives of the holy men, that one has a duty to the wider society. In *On Divine Love* he explains that Jesus' request to Peter to "Shepherd my sheep" (John 21.16) means that Jesus considered the care of his sheep the greatest service, which is a rather free interpretation of his words but one very much in keeping with Theodoret's own views.[32] We see this clearly in the case of Eusebius, who, although not ordained, shuts himself away but is persuaded by Ammianus that he has a duty to consider others and lead his community, which he does (*Religious History* 4.3). The other issue is that Theodoret also placed himself in the forefront as one of the best examples of a bishop.

The relationship between the monks of Syria and the clergy was a symbiotic one. The latter benefited from the inspirations to piety as practical, living examples of what it meant to live a holy life. The holy men in turn were nourished, often physically but also spiritually, by the men of the cloth. The clergy are seen as men of action and the ascetics as men of prayer. Rather than operating outside the sphere of the church, we see the ascetics as deferential to the hierarchy and considering themselves unworthy to join it. The church, on the other hand, was very keen to see that certain ones among them did. The clergy, in particular Theodoret, are the calm professionals, the ascetics, the enthusiastic amateurs. Theodoret was no ordinary bishop. His authority was peculiar to him, and the next chapter examines how this is described.

---

32. Εὐεργεσίαν δὲ μεγίστην ἡγοῦμαι τῶν ἐμῶν προβάτων τὴν ἐπιμέλειαν καὶ τὴν εἰς ἐκεῖνα κηδεμονίαν εἰς ἐμαυτὸν ἀναδέχομαι (but I consider care of my sheep to be the greatest service, and I accept for myself attention paid to them) (*On Divine Love* 10).

Chapter 11

Theodoret in the *Religious History*

It seems to me pretty clear that Blemmydes was convinced deep down that he was a saint.[1]

I would not go so far as to say that Theodoret thought the same about himself, but an acquaintance with the *Religious History* certainly reveals that he was very careful to portray himself in relentlessly glowing terms. The very presence of Theodoret in the *Religious History* is one of the most striking aspects of the work. Far from introducing himself accidentally or unconsciously, this presence is crucial to understanding the work as a whole. In some sense, he is referred to in every single life in that he ends each one in a uniform though not identical manner. The last chapter of each life always includes a plea that Theodoret, as the author, receive a blessing, intercession, help, or prayer from the ascetic about whom he has just written.[2] One could argue that this hardly constitutes a presence but is merely a sign of his consciousness of the demands of the genre. Or one could interpret this as Theodoret portraying himself as a devotee of these individuals.[3] This is what Theodoret tells us he is doing and, while this may be true or may be one element, it in no way explains the markedly positive image Theodoret draws for himself in the text.

He appears in more concrete form as a witness to the events he is

---

1. Munitiz 1981, 166. I recommend this short article as a good read, even for those who think they are not remotely interested in fourteenth-century Byzantine hagiography.

2. This formality is how Devos (1979) renumbered the lives and argued that two of them had been wrongly separated. Krueger (1997a) argues that by using very similar words each time Theodoret shows that he sees them as canonical gestures. He declares that Theodoret writing his *Religious History* is performing an act of piety similar to going on a pilgrimage (712). This is exactly what Theodoret would have us think. He virtually repeats it all the way through the text, though it is unclear how enlightening this is.

3. Referring to this phenomenon of ending each life with a plea for a blessing, Krueger remarks, a touch naively, "A rhetoric of piety is embedded in the *Religious History*'s structure" (1997a, 711).

describing in a remarkable number of instances, that is, in seventeen lives out of a total of twenty-eight.[4] So in almost two-thirds of the *Religious History*'s constituent parts Theodoret reports that he spoke to eyewitnesses or was an eyewitness himself. Indeed, he makes this claim for the whole of his work in the prologue (11) but he only makes direct reference to it in seventeen of the lives. In the other eleven, he simply asks for the ascetic's blessing at the end. So, for instance, he says that he was told about Eusebius by those who knew him (4.7–12); he heard about Publius from his followers (5.10); and he tells us that Jacob of Cyrrhestica told him about Symeon (6.3). He spoke to the subjects of nine of the lives (18, 20, 21, 22–23, 24–25, 26, 28, 29, 30).

The nature of his presence as a witness or a researcher varies enormously from life to life. In one, for instance, he says that he heard about Maësymas curing a child from the child's mother (*Religious History* 14.3). In the life of Jacob of Cyrrhestica, as we have seen, he is the major character in the long account second only to the ascetic (21). It is perhaps also worth noting that out of the first thirteen, that is, those holy men from the area around Antioch, he is a witness (or spoke to witnesses) for seven, and out of the fifteen from Cyrrhus he is a witness for ten. Of the twenty accounts of dead ascetics, he is a character in ten, but of the eight living he is there in all but one of the narratives. This is not surprising in that one would expect him to know more as he became an adult, and especially after becoming a bishop, for it would have been part of his work to know such individuals in his diocese.

It is not his presence in these lives that is remarkable, however, but the role he plays in the narratives, which is active and always very positive. One might see this as the church writing the history of asceticism with itself firmly in the position of authority. However, it appears that Theodoret is writing the account for himself rather than as a representative of the church.[5] This could perhaps be argued from those instances discussed earlier, but of unique interest is his introduction of himself as a child.[6] Theodoret mentions his childhood in four lives, those of Aphrahat (*Religious History* 8), Peter (9),

---

4. The lives in which he appears are 4, 5, 6, 8, 9, 12, 13, 14, 18, 20, 21, 22–23, 24–25, 26, 28, 29, and 30.

5. McLynn (1998) makes a similar point about Gregory Nazianzen.

6. In general, there is little about the childhood of his heroes.

Zeno (12), and Macedonius (13), almost the same narratives as the one in which his mother appears, which is natural. Before I go on to examine his portrayal of his young self, I wish to look at that of his mother.

Theodoret's Mother

She features in four different lives, those of Symeon the Elder (*Religious History* 6, not the stylite of the same name, who is the subject of life 26), Aphrahat (8), Peter (9), and Macedonius (13). The first glimpse we have of her is a very brief one at the end of the life of Symeon: "His blessing, while he was still alive, was enjoyed by my blessed and thrice-blessed mother, who often related to me many of the stories about him" (6.14). Theodoret neatly achieves several goals here. In case the reader might doubt his tale, he tells us the source of his account, which is of the highest order since it is his mother, who in turn is no ordinary woman but "blessed and thrice-blessed."[7] Describing one's mother in this way does two things: it shows Theodoret is a pious child, in the sense of showing his parent great respect; and it indicates that he came from worthy stock himself. It is very appropriate that the bishop of Cyrrhus should have a mother who is thrice blessed and has received the blessing of such a holy man. The reader finishes the life with enhanced trust and respect for its author.

The next time we meet Theodoret's mother is in the life of Aphrahat, the noble Persian who spoke only broken Greek (*Religious History* 8.2). Again, at the end of the life, Theodoret authenticates his account, telling us how he knows about this man. This time he says that as a youngster (μειράκιον)[8] he saw Aphrahat and received his blessing when he visited him with his mother (8.15). Here he says: "Half-opening the door to her, according to his wont, he honored her with conversation and blessing;" One might be forgiven for thinking that this is another instance of the author showing his character as a dutiful and respectful son, but once again he is doing more.

---

7. Ἡ μακαρία καὶ τρισμακαρία μου μήτηρ. Palladius, who devotes three chapters of his *Lausiac History* to Melania (46, 54, 55), also calls her thrice blessed.

8. A youth not yet twenty-one, according to Liddle and Scott (1968), or a teenager according to Lampe (1961). This is not the first time that Theodoret introduces himself into the narrative. He appears in the fourth life, that of Eusebius of Teleda.

He continues: "But me he received within and gave me a share in the wealth of his prayer." We learned two paragraphs earlier that women were not allowed inside his door (8.13), so this is no special insult to Theodoret's mother. It does illustrate sharply, however, that even as an adolescent he was more important than his mother or enjoyed more access to holy men than she did. One might remark that only modern readers would draw attention to this, for it would be taken for granted by an earlier audience. While allowing that attitudes have changed, it is surely interesting that Theodoret even comments on it in that case. And he does comment here and elsewhere (3.14, 3.22, 8.15, 26.21) that many holy men did not allow women near them. He is being quite explicit here that although he was young he had more access to this man than his mother did.

The two lives in which she plays a large part are those of Peter the Galatian (*Religious History* 9) and Macedonius (13). The first is the story of her conversion to a sober and pious life before the birth of Theodoret, and the second is the account of how it was through the intervention of Macedonius that her son was born. Blomfield Jackson, who has a keen eye for entertaining, begins his introduction to the works of Theodoret with a retelling of the vivid story of the visit to Peter by Theodoret's mother.[9] Before she met this holy man, she had cut a dashing figure, wearing expensive jewelry, fine clothes, and makeup, for, explains Theodoret, "she had not yet tasted the more perfect virtue" (9.6). She went to visit him because she had an eye infection that doctors could not cure. A friend told her that another woman, the wife of the comes orientis no less, had had the same complaint and been cured by means of a prayer and sign of the cross from Peter (9.5). Theodoret's mother went to the holy man, who rebuked her at length for her finery.

She was healed in both body and soul since Peter cured her eye and also her desire for adornment, even though, says Theodoret, she was only twenty-two and not yet a mother.[10] He adds that he was not born until seven years later and was her only child. It seems to me that he conveys a definite piece of information here: he is telling the

---

9. Jackson [1892] 1994, 1.

10. "Not impossibly the discontinuance of the use of cosmetics may have helped, if not caused, the cure" (ibid., 1). Martin of Tours also cured Paulinus of Nola, who had what sounds like a cataract (*Life of Martin of Tours* 19.3). Presumably cosmetics played no part in this.

reader that for seven years before he was born his mother lived modestly and piously. She had been glamorous once but had seen the error of her ways and, due to her encounter with Peter, had come to understand how she should live. She maintained this proper lifestyle for some years before her son was born.

Before telling this story Theodoret gives Peter an elaborate introduction, stressing his fame and the impossibility of doing justice to his achievements.[11] He then lets us know that he had a very special relationship with Peter because when he was a child he used to visit him. Peter would sit the child on his lap and feed him grapes and bread.[12] Theodoret notes that his mother took him to see the ascetic once a week and then goes on to the story of how she first came to know him.

Shortly after Theodoret's birth, his mother fell very ill. Again ordinary doctors were useless. Theodoret says that his nurse begged Peter to help her, which naturally he did. He simply came to her and prayed, and her fever ended and she recovered. Theodoret tells only one more anecdote about Peter before ending the narrative. This is the story in which Peter cuts a belt in two, putting half around his waist and giving the other portion to the child Theodoret.[13] Theodoret's mother took charge of it. He tells us that she used it, presumably placing it on the sufferer, when any member of the family fell sick. Neighbors borrowed this marvel to restore themselves to health. Eventually one failed to return it, which is why Theodoret no longer has it in his possession at the time of writing.

The story performs several functions. It illustrates the healing powers of Peter and indicates the special regard in which Theodoret

---

11. This is a topos in such literature (see Festugière 1960, 129–37).

12. "A scene like this takes us closer than do a hundred miracles to the appeal of the holy man in late Roman society" remarks Brown (1971, 435), although by now it should be clear that I am arguing for a less credulous view.

13. See Hill 2000, 6–7, 366, n. 6, on Theodoret describing God as wearing a belt and equating a belt with power. Theodoret says, quoting Psalm 65, "You make the mountains steady and immovable, you move the sea when you wish, and in turn cause it to rest so that there is not even a sound of it for those listening; you achieve each of these things by employing your ineffable and immeasurable power, which you wear like some belt. . . . Since, you see, one who is girt is better equipped for doing whatever one wishes, in figurative fashion he called God's power a belt" (366). Hill comments that this passage is evidence that someone apart from Theodoret has been at work here, emending and misreading ζώνη (belt) for ζωή (life). One might be inclined to argue, after reading the *Religious History,* that these are Theodoret's words.

was held by this ascetic. It is revealing of the authority of the mother in the family while also indirectly laying the blame for its loss with her since she had assumed the power to lend it to others, although Theodoret told us explicitly that it was a gift to him. I would argue, then, that Theodoret's mother is being shown as someone who saw the error of her ways and became the suitable parent of a future bishop. She is also someone with whom Theodoret implicitly compares himself, always to his own advantage. She is a pious individual and was responsible for Theodoret's extremely early introduction to the ascetics, but she was never Theodoret's equal in any respect.

The last life in which she occurs is that of Macedonius (*Religious History* 13), whom she supplied with his meager fare of soaked barley for many years (13.3). She appears very early in this life, and her function there is extremely interesting. Theodoret describes how Macedonius visited her when, again, she became sick. He learned that she was refusing food that would have helped in her recovery. Theodoret's explanation of her behavior is that she had already embraced the ascetic life. The holy man, in what I would argue is an extremely important speech, rebukes her. He says that he himself had felt weak the previous day and so had taken some bread, although he had eaten only barley for forty years. Had he not taken the food necessary to keep himself alive he could have been charged with preferring death from hunger to the philosophic life. Indeed, he carries on, he would like Theodoret's mother to bring him bread in the future. Theodoret writes this in direct speech, which is justifiable, one supposes, since his mother had heard the words. He goes on to comment that this proves that Macedonius had eaten only barley for forty years.

But the speech tells us more than that. It is a criticism of carrying asceticism to extremes and argues that one should eat in moderation. But, cleverly, it cannot be accused of being a disparagement of holy men since these are the words of an ascetic directed toward Theodoret's mother. So she becomes not only the representation of a vain woman who saw the error of her ways in the life of Peter (*Religious History* 9) but of a vain ascetic carrying her self-mortification too far. I would not suggest that Theodoret wishes to condemn his mother, but a point is made diplomatically by making her the object of criticism rather than one of the holy men. It is extreme ascetic practices that Theodoret censures, and we see him exercising a moderating influence on such extremes later in the work in the life of Jacob of Cyrrhestica.

However, the real drama concerning Theodoret's mother in this life is the story of his conception, which one might almost be forgiven for calling the climax of the narrative. Theodoret relates various anecdotes, revealing the power and influence of the holy man, and concludes with the circumstances of his birth. His parents had been married for thirteen years with no children (*Religious History* 13.16). His mother, whom Theodoret describes as sterile, was not distressed, believing that this was God's will. His father had a more conventional view of the situation and begged servants of God (οἵ θεῖοι θεράποντες) to pray for children for him. They all agreed to pray, but Macedonius promised that his request would be successful. Three years later, as no child was yet forthcoming, Theodoret's father went back to Macedonius, who told him to send his wife to him. When Theodoret's mother went to the holy man, he told her that she should dedicate her child to God. She made the rather indirect reply that she wished only for spiritual salvation. This was clearly a good answer since Macedonius said in that case—that is, because her request was pious—she would be doubly rewarded by being given a son.[14] And a year later Theodoret was born.

Theodoret prolongs the story a little longer with the addition of the scare of a miscarriage. His mother sent for Macedonius, who came and reminded her of her promise to give the child to God. She replied that she would rather not give birth at all than fail to give her offspring to God. With that, she and her child were saved. As one might expect, we learn more about Theodoret than his mother. The whole episode is only two paragraphs long (13.16–17), and yet Theodoret demonstrates that his existence was not a matter of chance. He had to be prayed for several times, and his mother had to promise to give him to God. When the time came for him to be born, she was reminded of this promise and had to give it anew. His mother is completely passive: while childless, she accepted her lot as the will of God; when pregnant, she readily agreed to Macedonius's request that she devote any child to God and she reiterated her submission to divine will when miscarriage threatened. She behaves, in short, as

---

14. Modern readers may balk at this but rather hypocritically since even today it is hardly unheard of for boys to be treated preferentially.

any decent Christian woman should and is a faultless mother for a remarkable bishop.

This is the last appearance of Theodoret's mother in the *Religious History*. She gives birth to Theodoret and immediately disappears from sight. In this she corresponds very neatly to females of Greek myth, who also drop out of the narrative once they have given birth.[15] Macedonius is the last holy man from the vicinity of Antioch, so perhaps it would be unlikely that Theodoret would mention his mother again since from now on he discusses the holy men from around Cyrrhus. However, one cannot escape the impression that the structure is deliberately dramatic since we are supposed to be reading about these ascetics in chronological order. It therefore seems unexpected that the last one to die from the area of Antioch would be one so involved with Theodoret's parents several years before he was born. After all, he does feature as a child and youth in several of the lives preceding that of Macedonius. Whether or not the arrangement is deliberate, the effect is almost theatrical. Theodoret is born, and his mother vanishes from view. So does his father, but he had never been very prominent anyway, appearing only in this life of Macedonius. It is a common feature of saints generally that they often have close links with their mothers and much more remote fathers.[16]

Theodoret's mother is mentioned in any discussion of Theodoret's life as an important influence on the religious development of her son.[17] It is entirely appropriate to her role in the narrative that we do not even learn her name. She is there because she is Theodoret's mother. Virtually no other woman is named in the text, so in this she is unexceptional. As with hagiography generally, one is on much firmer ground drawing conclusions about Theodoret and the impact he wishes to have on his readers than about any of the figures about whom he is writing.[18] He is composing a narrative reminiscent of the Gospels.[19] He tells of the time before his birth, the preparations for

---

15. This is discussed by Lefkowitz (1981, 41–47). See also Lefkowitz 1986 and Buxton 1994, 121.

16. Browning 1981, 121, 123.

17. See, for instance, Canivet 1977, 46, 52–53; and Price 1985a, xi.

18. Coon 1997, xxi–xii.

19. See Krueger 1997b, esp. 416–18, which demonstrates how Theodoret draws parallels between his work and the Bible. Krueger draws the rather startling conclusion:

it, the piety of his mother, and the difficulties she encounters before he can be born. One cannot help but be reminded of the birth of Jesus.[20] Theodoret's tale is perhaps not in this category, but he is surely contributing to a justification of the meaning of his name ("gift of God").

It is interesting to contrast Theodoret's mother with Monica, the mother of Augustine.[21] Monica remained constant while her son underwent a conversion.[22] Here Theodoret is constant while his mother is converted to a pious life in preparation for her son. Like Monica, it is virtually impossible to assess how much of the real woman can be accessed from her son's portrait. Theodoret's mother, like Monica, is there to perform a function for her son. She is a literary construct and an echo of a more famous mother, Mary.

The parallel with the Gospels is continued in the picture Theodoret gives us of himself as a child. In the life of Aphrahat, who performed miracles (*Religious History* 8.9, 11, 13, 14), he was blessed by that holy man while still an adolescent. As was discussed in chapter 9, this man let Theodoret but not his mother into his cell, so even at this age he is being recognized as special. In the next life, that of Peter, Theodoret again appears as a child. He describes the holy man's companion, Daniel, who had been possessed by a demon and came to Peter to be exorcised. Once cured, the man stayed as

---

"Theodoret no doubt understood his portraits of the saints as a mimesis of God's work, both as a revelation of the heights attainable by those fashioned by God in God's image, but also to the extent that in writing his text, Theodoret's work was analogous to God's work, since both Theodoret and God were sorts of painters" (418). I am not sure I would want to accuse Theodoret of such hubris myself.

20. See Patlagean 1983, 105, 107–8, on the use of the scriptural model for hagiography. For a parallel with Theodoret, see the *Life of Theodore of Sykeon* (148), where the author describes how his parents were childless for several years. They came to the saint, who prayed over them, which solved this condition and the author was born. The child entered the monastery and became a disciple. Despite the similarities in the stories, the function is very different and is merely here to vouch for the authenticity of the account. As remarked earlier, Cox (1983, 34) distinguishes between the biographies of sons of gods and merely godlike individuals, observing that only the former have miraculous birth stories. She also remarks that they alone work miracles. Theodoret works no miracles, but the monks closest to him do (see chapter 7).

21. On the problems of understanding her, see, most recently, Clark 1999.

22. Richard Price has observed that I exaggerate the contrasts, and it is true that Augustine tells us that his mother was addicted to drink in her youth (*Confessions* 9.8). However, when she interacts with Augustine I would argue that she is a force in favor of orthodoxy and perhaps could be seen as representing his conscience. Theodoret's mother plays no such role since we never see her interact with her adult son.

a follower out of gratitude, and Theodoret says he knew this man and that he himself remembers the miracle. It is not entirely clear what he means by this, as he does not say he saw it himself (τοῦ θαύματος μέμνημαι), but he does specify that he saw the price paid for the cure (καὶ τὸν τῆς θεραπείας ἐθεασάμην μισθόν, 9.4). Theodoret says that he heard the two men speaking about him and Daniel said that Theodoret would share in the noble service of him (ὡς τῆς καλῆς αὐτῷ ταύτης διακονίας κοινωνήσω), presumably meaning that Theodoret, too, would join Peter's entourage. Peter said he thought this would not happen, as Theodoret's parents loved him too much to allow it.[23] Theodoret then adds the scene of Peter sitting him on his lap and putting grapes and bread into his mouth and tells us that his mother brought him to the holy man every week to receive his blessing, thus illustrating the love both his mother and Peter had for him. Peter also gave him the belt (9.15) discussed earlier.

The next time we meet the young Theodoret is in the life of Zeno (*Religious History* 12), and the episode is a strange one. To give an idea of Zeno's character, Theodoret recounted an anecdote about this man's water supply. Zeno was very insistent that he would fetch his own water and did not want anyone else to carry it for him. When a well-meaning but clearly irritating person insisted on bringing him some, Zeno poured the water out and went back to fetch some more. Theodoret went to search out this holy man, who had an unusual career, as he had been in the imperial service as a postman before leaving to live in a tomb on a mountain near Antioch.[24] Theodoret climbed the mountain and found a man holding water jars. Theodoret asked if he knew where the wonderful Zeno lived. The man replied that he had no knowledge of anyone by that name, and this, mysteriously, was enough for Theodoret to guess that he was speaking to the man himself.[25] The youthful Theodoret then seems to have simply followed the man into his dwelling and asked questions about

---

23. This might confirm Lane Fox's view that being "dumped" in a monastery as a child indicates a lack of parental love (1997, 217–18). He suggests that Daniel's withdrawal from human society later in life was due to this emotional deprivation as a child.

24. Price points out that this means he was one of the *agentes in rebus,* the civil servants with responsibility for the public post (1985a, 99, n. 3).

25. From the account, it would seem that Theodoret deduced this fact from the water jars in his hand.

philosophy, which Zeno answered.[26] After a long time Theodoret decided to return home and asked the holy man for a blessing. This was refused because, said Zeno, Theodoret, as a reader (*reader,* as in the office in the church), should rather bless him. Theodoret pointed out that this was inappropriate since he was still very young ("for I had only just experienced a slight growth of down," [12.4]). He added that if Zeno forced him on this he, Theodoret, would not come to visit again! One of these arguments did the trick, and the ascetic reluctantly blessed Theodoret. Similarly, Jacob (21.32), Limnaeus (22.3), and Eusebius (18.3) could all be described as antisocial, going out of their way to avoid human intercourse, except with Theodoret. In all three cases, the ascetics take pleasure in his company, it would seem almost exclusively.

The short episode about Zeno tells us much about Theodoret. Even as a teenager he went seeking out holy men and shows himself a shrewd judge of the ascetic mind. He is concerned to learn from them and in turn is received with much respect. The man does not turn him away but rather considers that he ought to receive a blessing from someone much his junior. Zeno is portrayed as showing immense respect for the church when he considers that even a very young reader has precedence over himself, and Theodoret is careful to say how young he was.[27] Such deference demonstrates Zeno's piety. It also portrays Theodoret as being shown immense respect even when very young and inexperienced. Surely here we are seeing a version of the child prodigy so common in hagiography, where saints do not have typical childhoods but have wisdom beyond their years.[28]

Macedonius's role in Theodoret's birth has already been described. This particular holy man, we are told, is very famous and the equal in virtue to all the preceding ascetics in the introduction to his life. The last chapter deals with his funeral, which "all the citizens and aliens, and those entrusted to administer the great offices' attended. Theodoret, though, claims a special knowledge of him, which he reveals after describing several healings and a prophecy made by this admirable man. He describes the circumstances sur-

---

26. Dagron 1970, 259 n. 52. See also "Monachisme" in Viller, Cavallera, and de Guibert 1980, col. 1556.
27. Canivet 1977, 45–46.
28. Browning 1981, 120–21.

rounding his conception and the threat of a miscarriage, which the holy man averted, but before ending he gives us a vignette starring himself and Macedonius. The latter says:

You were born, my child, with much toil: I spent many nights begging this alone of God, that your parents should earn the name they received after your birth. So live a life worthy of this toil. Before you were born, you were offered up in promise. Offerings to God are revered by all, and are not to be touched by the multitude: so it is fitting that you do not admit the base impulses of the soul, but perform, speak and desire those things alone that serve God, the giver of the laws of virtue. (*Religious History* 13.18)

Theodoret comments modestly that although he has not managed to fulfill these wishes yet he prays for divine help to do so during the rest of his life. This is the last we hear of Theodoret the child. Curiously enough, it is also the life in which he is born. After this life come those from Cyrrhus, and we only see Theodoret as a bishop.

Theodoret is present in the work to show that he can personally vouch for the stories he is telling, which might otherwise seem almost too remarkable, as he himself maintains in the prologue (10). The work is very studiedly local, and there are references to Cyrrhus even in the first thirteen lives (e.g., *Religious History* 2.21 and 3.1). But when he is present, he is very seldom there merely as a witness, in contrast to the other works of the genre. He is shown not just respect by the holy men but immense respect, which is unusual, and he makes this explicit each time in case the reader might not notice.

In the previous chapter we saw the way in which Eusebius of Asikha (*Religious History* 18.2), Maris, (20.4), Jacob of Cyrrhestica (21), Limnaeus (22.3), and Jacob of Nimouza (25.2) all gave tokens of their extraordinary esteem for Theodoret. These could all be marks of respect that were due to a bishop, but with the introduction of Theodoret as a child it is impossible to ignore the very personal authority he is building for himself in this work. It is possible to see his role developing in these four lives. In the first, Aphrahat, who had even addressed an emperor, shows the child more honor than his mother. In the second we see Peter giving him a belt with curing powers as well as showing special affection for him. Zeno asks the teenaged reader to bless him, and there are explicit honors forecast for him by Macedonius. This is no ordinary bishop but one divinely ordained.

When one considers the attributes normally shared by saints and then reads the *Religious History* it is a little bewildering to realize that the author himself has several. Many saints' lives are modeled on that of Jesus, which presents several of the usual features: the special birth, the close maternal link and a distant father, the precocious childhood, miracles (Theodoret did not perform any, but he witnessed or was the beneficiary of them), and struggles with demons (a demon spoke to him in the life of Jacob of Cyrrhestica). Many saints have visions. Theodoret does not have one, but Jacob does on his behalf when John the Baptist, no less, vouches for Theodoret.

Theodoret is central to the *Religious History*. The thread running through the work is that of Theodoret's life, which, being woven into the tapestry of the lives of holy men, takes on a sanctified hue. After reading his work, the reader cannot fail to remember that his very name means "gift of God."

Chapter 12

The Representation of
the Ascetics

If the interpretation of Theodoret as a remarkable church leader is correct, this must affect how his heroes are to be seen. He purports after all to be holding them up as paragons of virtue, as leaders to follow. If they follow his leadership instead, it is necessary to consider how he intended his readers to interpret them.

Holy men are portrayed as self-denying, suffering, and passive. They are so pious that they have acquired supernatural powers. This is a gift God bestowed upon them as a reward for their self-control, their conquering of normal bodily desires for sex, warmth, food, or comfort of any kind. Indeed, often they have to be protected against their own enthusiasm in carrying out God's wishes. So, for instance, we see Theodoret practicing a little deceit in order to persuade Jacob not to make himself more ill than he already is (*Religious History* 21.6–7). In other words, he is showing the reader that the holy men are malleable, at least by Theodoret because they have so much respect for him.

Church writers often blended masculine and feminine characteristics in these saints' lives in order to show the otherworldly nature of Christian sanctity.[1] It seems to me that we can see something similar going on here; Theodoret's holy men have the characteristics of virtuous women. Self-denial, suffering, and passivity have often been considered the lot of women. If this seems hard to accept, then Theodoret makes it easier by expressing it himself in a striking passage. In the life

---

1. Coon 1997, xviii–xx.

of Acepsimas he says that people such as his hero do not care about men's praise:

> Instead, they transferred all their love to the Bridegroom, like modest women who are eager to be loved and praised by their spouses but despise adulation from others. Because of this the Bridegroom made them celebrated even against their will. (*Religious History* 15.6)

In their relationship with Christ these men are like women, like dutiful wives whose only concern is to please their husbands. This could perhaps be dismissed as colorful language, and it is indeed vivid. But it is not the only instance. In the treatise *On Divine Love* there is a similar equation with women in a quotation from Paul ("I have yoked you to one husband to present a pure virgin to God" [2 Cor 11.2]), although this is a more general point. More specific, in the life of Aphrahat the hero compares himself to a woman. He explains to the emperor, Valens, that he has come to help in the struggle against heresy because it is an emergency.

> If I had been a girl shut away in some inner room and saw a fire attack my father's house, what would you have advised me to do on seeing the flames kindled and the house on fire?[2] (8.8)

Even a girl, who would normally be hidden away from the public gaze and remain passive, would be justified in taking action here. Similarly, even holy men who wish only to contemplate God sometimes have to commit a feat of bravery. Antony had said that monks who leave their solitude and exist among ordinary men are like fish out of water (*Life of Antony* 85), so the assumption is that in the normal course of events they do not interact with the outside world. But if there is an emergency they come to help.

If we accept the representation of holy men as women then some instances are more chilling than others. Salamanes is completely passive, one might even say comatose (*Religious History* 19). He never moves or speaks, just lies in a hole in the ground. He does not perform miracles but is considered so holy that rival villages snatch

---

2. On heresy as fire, see Eusebius's *Life of Constantine* (2.61) and Socrates' *Ecclesiastical History* (1.6.1–2).

and reclaim him without any response on his part. He is ordained, but there is no reaction from him. All this is held up as admirable, and Theodoret says in the final paragraph: "Thus, he had made himself totally dead to this life."[3] One might wonder at this model.

In the prologue Theodoret described how normal perceptions change with asceticism so that pain may seem like pleasure.

> Therefore, these who have followed the path of life through innumerable labours and broken the body in with sweat and toil, who have not experienced the passion of laughter but spent all their life in mourning and tears, who have deemed fasting Sybaritic nourishment, laborious vigil a most pleasant sleep, the hard resistance of the ground a soft couch, a life of prayer and psalmody a pleasure measureless and insatiable, these who have attained every form of virtue — who would not rightly admire them? (Prologue 7)

It is not clear whether one can extrapolate his views on women from his views on holy men. That is, if we accept that holy men have female characteristics, can this tell us something about his attitude toward women? If so, the passage just cited perhaps has alarming consequences.

Like women, holy men are there to serve. This may or may not correspond to reality, but it is the picture Theodoret is choosing to paint. In his work they are pious individuals who can be influenced and will help in an emergency. They are mavericks, and they do act independently, but not independently of the church or Theodoret. They need guidance for their own good, even for their own survival, guidance that people like Theodoret can give. Just as women need men to show them what to do, so holy men need Theodoret.

How close or faithful are the representations of these ascetics to reality? It is impossible to know. Almost as undiscernible for modern scholars is the exact role or function such individuals played in late antique society.[4] Yet to demand such clarity is perhaps to ask the wrong questions given the nature of the evidence. After all, there is much still to be discovered since we do have access to the roles and functions authors such as Theodoret ascribed to the monks. We can

---

3. See MacDermot 1971, 27, on the ascetic being dead to the world, having left society and his possessions.

4. See Frank 2000, 2–3, for similar provisos on reading pilgrims' tales.

determine what impression they wished to leave with those who read or heard their texts. In some ways, this is more important since texts can and do influence behavior and views. Whatever the original motives and actions of holy men, it is the way in which others described and reported them that affected both subsequent exemplars and observers. Writers help to shape the ideas, perhaps one might say the ideology, of their day.

Certainly the writing of saints' lives has long been recognized as contributing to and forming the ideas of the saints and their relationship with the church. It is evident that the church saw the need to write about these individuals, who may in their own day have been rebellious and troublesome figures, to write them into the history and body of the church. A work such as the *Religious History* is not merely meant to record events or people but to fashion and create a world for others. This is not to suggest that Theodoret was fabricating any of his material but merely to comment on the creative, and hugely influential, power of the written word.

Similarly, we have no access to the actual relationship Theodoret had with these individuals, only to a description of how he wished readers to see it. It is true that he presents us with a rather contradictory picture, but this is not really surprising. First, he wanted his heroes to be strong and independent (and worth reading and writing about), but, second, he also wished to present them as deferring to himself. He does present himself as respectful and admiring of these paragons of virtue because his intention is that his readers should leave the text in a similar frame of mind. He also claims to be holding the ascetics up for his readers to emulate. And it was safe to describe and praise the occasional bout of parrhesia since being deprived of sleep, food, and sex would in the real world tend to lead to the opposite behavior. But crucial for his composition of the work is his representation of himself as powerful and influential in Syria.[5]

Ascetics are presented as founts of holiness to be tapped into, channeled, used, and directed by those with the necessary knowledge and authority. Or, to use another analogy, they are the foot-

---

5. Norris makes a similar point about Gregory Nazianzen's oration about Basil, in which there is a tension between praising his subject and his own image: "Subtext and text, Gregory's reputation and Basil's honor, are occasionally at war" (2000, 149). See also Konstan (2000, 161), who reflects on the relationship between the writer and his or her subject.

soldiers who fight the bishops' battles. And Theodoret did have battles to be fought. It may initially seem unclear how they were to be useful to Theodoret in his war of words with the Alexandrian church, but when one considers the role played by monks on behalf of the Egyptians, Theodoret's undertaking seems timely. He needed to show that Syria had troops of equal fervor and frightening determination. His stress on communities also makes good sense in this connection; it was beneficial for the Christian message to describe large numbers of devotees. Equally, it would be alarming for those inimical to the Antiochenes to read about swarms of wild barbarians who owed their allegiance to a fierce stylite, who in turn was loyal and respectful only to his bishop.

Conclusion

When I began my work on the *Religious History* my main focus was on Theodoret and the attitudes he revealed in the work, the picture he was trying to paint for his audience, and why he included a self-portrait, and such a positive one at that, in so many of the lives. The ascetics who are the subject of the *Religious History* are startling in their own right, however, and deserve their own study. For some reason, the interpretation of the holy man as patron, intercessor, counselor, or even teacher did not seem to me to capture their most important aspect. Those attributes seemed rather to be merely by-products of their singular status. These people were trying to flee the madding crowd, rather than become important participants in it. They were men and women going off to fight their own demons and achieve a better life in whatever way we choose to interpret *better.* They clearly felt it would be better. They were individuals who gave up all material goods and endured every type of adversity for their beliefs. It was not difficult to see why people might respect them even when they could not follow their example. Nor was it difficult to understand that others might feel they had achieved some level of wisdom due to all their privations.

They thought for themselves, were defiant toward authority, defended the poor against the rich, and had total disregard for worldly honors. They also rejected the version of Christianity available to the rest of society. As Chadwick observes, "From the third century the question was being put with steadily increasing pressure whether the Church could occupy a position of influence in high society without losing something of its moral power and independence."[1] Clearly,

---

1. Chadwick 1967, 175.

more and more people thought not. A substantial number of individuals adopted a way of life radically different from the vast majority of society precisely at the time when Christianity was receiving imperial acceptance and approval. Such people can be seen, and indeed often were seen, as rebels. Just how far their rebellion took them is difficult to say, given that we seldom have sources sympathetic to those rebelling against the system.

We do know, however, of some instances in this period that can give us a clue as to how far these mavericks could go. Monks mobbed and attacked the pagan governor of Alexandria, Orestes, wounding him in the process (Socrates, *Ecclesiastical History* 7.14). In North Africa the Circumcellions, described by Brown as "the extreme wing of the Donatist church," seem to have had social reform as an end and used violence as a means of achieving it.[2] People who took the Gospels literally had the potential to be highly antiestablishment. "I did not come to bring peace but a sword," says Jesus in Matthew 10.34. In Luke 18.22 one reads, as Symeon heard, "Sell all you have and give it to the poor," and a little later there is the warning to the upper classes that "It is easier for a camel to pass through the eye of a needle than for a rich man to enter the kingdom of heaven" (Luke 18.25). These are nothing if not revolutionary statements.[3] People who took them literally could be a threat to the established church, and it is clear from the canons of Chalcedon that it was recognized that monks had to be controlled.

On the other hand, the fiery zeal of the holy men had the potential to be a beneficial resource if aimed in the desired direction. They could be valuable allies, as the bishops of Alexandria discovered. If their energy could be harnessed for the church, they could be tolerated. One way of harnessing it was to ordain them and make them priests, without insisting that they perform any pastoral duties, as we have seen Theodoret record. Such ordinations brought them directly into the hierarchy of the church. Their ordination was perhaps their subordination. Another solution was to write hagiographies about them, portraying them as defying everyone except bishops. Since it was not simply a question of the holy men themselves but also the

---

2. Brown 1967, 229 (see also 335). See Augustine (*Epistle* 185) for an extended, if one-sided, description of their activities, which Brown describes as comparable to the accounts in English newspapers of the Irish peasant agitation.

3. For a clear and convincing exposition of the way pagan and Christian ascetics were transformed from rebels to supporters of the status quo, see Francis 1995, 181–89.

influence they had over others, which could be either dangerous or beneficial, the church had to be, and indeed was, extremely adept at defusing rebellion and diverting the fervor of the monks to its service. Theodoret's work is a very clear example of such diversion. Simply by writing about these people he was building a reputation of power for himself by portraying them as deferring to himself. As Hobbes remarked, "reputation of power is power because it draws with it the adherence of those that need protection."[4]

Chadwick comments, "By the end of the fourth century the Church had virtually captured society. In worldly terms of status and social influence, the episcopate of even moderately important cities had become an established career to which a man might aspire for reasons not exclusively religious."[5] Bishops in the fourth and fifth centuries wielded power because the church, as an institution, had become phenomenally wealthy and influential, but it is salutary to note that most bishops from this period are now forgotten. Bishops were more likely to be influential if their sees were imperial or provincial capitals, important trading centers, or the traditional homes of the wealthiest and oldest families in the empire. Many of the bishops whose names we remember were the incumbents of the major sees of the empire, places like Rome, Milan, Constantinople, Jerusalem, Antioch, and Alexandria.

Cyrrhus was not in this league. Theodoret's family was from the elite but not prominent enough to ensure him a major see. We do not possess enough information about his background to assess how much it was responsible for his position in history. He certainly possessed as good an education as any in the empire, but there is more to him than that. Today his influence is largely due to the mass of writings he left, and although the *Religious History* has largely been overlooked as an object of study it has always been consulted for the information it provides about the author's early life and his connections to the ascetics of his area. Some of these were influential in church politics in their own right.

In the *Religious History* Theodoret laid the foundation for his reputation of power. With it, he helped yoke the energy of Syrian asceticism to drive himself forward. The text is usually mined for

---

4. See Hobbes [1651] 1958, 78. Hobbes is quoted in Brown (1982, 162; a variant is quoted on 181) to describe the Byzantine holy man.

5. Chadwick 1967, 174.

information on Syria, holy men, or Theodoret himself. It is extremely edifying in all three areas. It is an attempt to give Syria a standing equal to that of Egypt, to show that it produced prodigies of asceticism, individuals capable and prepared to go to extraordinary lengths out of love of God. The Syrians had lost ground to the Egyptians in the fifth century. They had seen the Syrian bishops of Constantinople, men such as John Chrysostom and Nestorius, destroyed by the Alexandrian bishops working in conjunction with monks. At least this is how church historians have portrayed the situation. It was necessary therefore to show that Syria had monks every bit as dedicated and holy as those of Egypt.

Theodoret was also a cleric. His monks were very much within the church, not apart from it or against it. At least this is how he portrayed them. They showed deference to priests and bishops, declined the priesthood as being too onerous, although the very best of their ranks were appointed bishop. Theodoret not only was a bishop but a bishop personally engaged in the titanic struggle against the Alexandrians. He knew his own position was under threat and skillfully, if not ultimately successfully, buttressed his reputation with this work. He did not write it to curry favor with the holy men but to parade his own power and influence with these people to show that they bowed to the authority of the Syrian church and especially to him. It was in his interest to glorify their position in his writing because the more remarkable they were the higher his own status would be.

Theodoret's authority was due in part to his episcopal rank, but it was also personal. He had known some of the holy men all his life. These ascetics raised the dead, exorcised demons, cured paralysis, defeated Persians with mosquitoes, rebuked emperors, defied governors, and lived for years in prayer and discomfort, but they were deferential to Theodoret. They had prayed for his birth, sat him on their laps, talked philosophy with him, received Communion from him, and sent their admirers to him for his blessing. He in turn cared for them, visited them, and gave them an enduring monument to their virtue in his *Religious History.*

In so doing, he also portrayed himself as someone in charge of pious monks. Access to the actual relationship Theodoret had with the ascetics of Syria, as opposed to the one he describes, must remain closed. We may speculate from the works he has left us, but it will always remain speculation. That in no way detracts from the importance of the text since in it he has drawn our attention to the anxieties and concerns of a bishop of his day. Some of the individuals spoke only Syriac, but Theodoret spoke their language as well as that of the ruling classes. He was a mediator between Greek and Syrian, rich and poor, ordinary and divine, few and many. The Syrian monks were his friends as well as friends of God. Theodoret needed as many allies as he could get. He was beset by enemies. This work has proved to be one of his most effective allies for posterity. Perhaps it was also responsible for his reinstatement in 451. Hobbes lists other constituents of power, one of which was eloquence.[6] Theodoret earned his reputation for power in large part by means of his eloquence. This is no dismissal at all of his activities but rather an acknowledgment of the power of the word, perhaps a reminder Christians do not need. Texts and the writing of them do not merely record events but influence them, and Theodoret's *Religious History* illustrates the power of the word very effectively. Much more could be written about Syria, holy men, and Theodoret, but I leave this to others, calling upon Sulpicius's eloquence to end my study.

> But now the book demands an end and I must conclude this account, not because I have exhausted all there is to say about Martin but because like those lazy poets who write carelessly at the end of their work, we are giving up, overwhelmed by the amount of material.
>
> —Sulpicius Severus, *Life of Martin of Tours*

---

6. "Eloquence is power, because it is seeming prudence" (Hobbes [1651] 1958, 79).

Bibliography

Adnès, A., and P. Canivet. 1967. "Guérisons miraculeuses et exorcisme dans l'*Histoire Philothée* de Théodoret." *Revue de l'Histoire des Religions* 171: 53–82.

Agrain, R. 1953. *L'Hagiographie: Ses sources, ses methodes, son histoire.* Poitiers.

Altaner, B., and A. Stuiber. 1978. *Patrologie.* Freiburg.

Ashbrook Harvey, S. 1988. "The Sense of a Stylite: Perspectives on Simeon the Elder." *Vigiliae Christianae* 42:376–94.

———. 1999. "Olfactory Knowing: Signs of Smell in the Vitae of Simeon Stylites." In *After Bardaisan,* G. J. Reinink and A. C. Klugkist, 23–34. Leuven.

———. 2000. "Antioch and Christianity." In *Antioch: The Lost City,* ed. Christine Kondoleon, 39–49. Princeton.

Azéma, Y. 1955–65. *Théodoret de Cyr: Correspondence.* Vols. 1–3. Paris.

———. 1984. "Sur la date de la mort de Théodoret de Cyr." *Pallas* 31:137–55.

Bacht, H. 1973. "Die Rolle des orientalischen Mönchtums in des kirchen-politischen Auseinandersetzungen um Chalkedon, 431–419." In *Das Konzil von Chalkedon: Geschichte und Gegenwart II,* ed. A. Grillmeier and H. Bacht, 4:193–314. Würzburg.

Bagnall, R. S. 1993. *Egypt in Late Antiquity.* Princeton.

Bammel, C. P. 1996. "Problems of the *Historia Monachorum.*" *Journal of Theological Studies,* n.s., 47:92–104.

Bardenhewer, O. 1924. *Geschichte der altkirchlichen Literatur.* Vol. 4. Freiburg.

Bardy, G. 1948a. "Les débuts du Nestorianisme (428–433)." In *Histoire de l'Eglise: De la mort de Théodose à l'élection de Grégoire le Grande,* ed. A. Fliche and V. Martin, 4:163–96.

———. 1948b. *La question des langues dans l'Eglise ancienne.* Vol. 1. Paris.

Barnes, T. D. 1986. "Angel of Light or Mystic Initiate? The Problem of the *Life of Antony.*" *Journal of Theological Studies,* n.s., 37:353–67.

———. 1993. *Athanasius and Constantius.* Cambridge, Mass.

Barton, T. S. 1994. *Power and Knowledge: Astrology, Physiognomics, and Medicine under the Roman Empire.* Ann Arbor.

Bergjan, S.-P. 1994. *Theodoret von Cyrus und der Neunizänismus.* Berlin.

Binns, John. 1994. *Ascetics and Ambassadors of Christ: The Monasteries of Palestine, 314–631.* Oxford.

Blockley, R. C. 1998. "The Dynasty of Theodosius." In Cameron and Garnsey 1998, 111–37.

Bowersock, G. W. 1990. *Hellenism in Late Antiquity.* Cambridge.

———. 1994. *Fiction as History: Nero to Julian.* Berkeley.

———. 2000. "The Syriac Life of Rabbula and Syrian Hellenism." In Hägg and Rousseau 2000a, 255–71.

Bowersock, G. W., P. R. L. Brown, and O. Grabar, eds. 1999. *Late Antiquity.* Cambridge, Mass.

Bowman, A. K., and G. Woolf, eds. 1994. *Literacy and Power in the Ancient World.* Cambridge.

Brakke, D. 1995. *Athanasius and the Politics of Asceticism.* Oxford.

Brock, S. 1982. "From Antagonism to Assimilation: Syriac Attitudes to Greek Learning." In *East of Byzantium: Syria and Armenia in the Formative Period,* ed. N. G. Garsoian, T. F. Matthews, and R. W. Thomson, 17–34. Washington, D.C.

———. "Early Christian Asceticism." In *Syriac Perspectives on Late Antiquity,* ed. S. Brock. London.

———. 1994. "Greek and Syriac in Late Antique Syria." In Bowman and Woolf 1994, 149–60.

———. "Syriac Culture, 337–425." In Cameron and Garnsey 1998, 708–19.

Brock, S., and S. Ashbrook Harvey. 1987. *Holy Women of the Syrian Orient.* Berkeley.

Brown, P. R. L. 1967. *Augustine of Hippo.* London.

———. 1971a. "The Rise and Function of the Holy Man in Late Antiquity." *Journal of Roman Studies* 61:80–101. Reprinted in Brown 1982, 103–52.

———. 1971b. *The World of Late Antiquity.* London.

———. 1976a. "Town, Village, and Holy Man: The Case of Syria." In *Assimilation et résistance à la culture gréco-romaine dans le monde ancien,* ed. D. M. Pippidi, 213–20. Bucharest. Reprinted in Brown 1982, 153–65.

———. 1976b. "Eastern and Western Christendom in Late Antiquity: A Parting of the Ways." In *The Orthodox Churches and the West: Studies in Church History,* 13:1–24. Oxford. Reprinted in Brown 1982, 166–95.

———. 1980. "The Philosopher and Society in Late Antiquity." In *The Center for Hermeneutical Studies in Hellenistic and Modern Culture, Protocol of the Thirty-fourth Colloquy, 1978,* 1–17. Berkeley.

———. 1982. *Society and the Holy in Late Antiquity.* London.

———. 1992. *Power and Persuasion.* Madison.

———. 1998a. "The Rise and Function of the Holy Man in Late Antiquity, 1971–97." *Journal of Early Christian Studies* 6.3: 353–76.

———. 1998b. "Asceticism: Pagan and Christian." In Cameron and Garnsey 1998, 601–31.

Browning, R. 1981. "The 'low level' saint's life in the early Byzantine world." In Hackel 1981, 117–27.

Buck, D. F. 1976. "The Structure of the *Lausiac History.*" *Byzantion* 46:292–307.

Bundy, D. 1991. "Jacob of Nisibis as a Model for the Episcopacy." *Le Muséon* 104:235–59.

Burridge, R. A. 1992. *What Are the Gospels?* Cambridge.

Buxton, R. 1994. *Imaginary Greece.* Cambridge.

Bynum, Caroline Walker. 1995. *The Resurrection of the Body in Western Christianity, 200–1336.* New York.

Cabrol, F. 1907. *Dictionnaire d'Archéologie Chrétienne et de Liturgie.* Vol. 14, pt. 1. Paris.

Cameron, Alan. 1993. *The Greek Anthology.* Oxford.

Cameron, Averil. 1989. "Virginity as Metaphor: Women and the Rhetoric of Early Christianity." In *History as Text: The Writing of Ancient History,* ed. Averil Cameron, 181–205. London.

———. 1991. *Christianity and the Rhetoric of Empire.* Berkeley.

———. 1993a. *The Later Roman Empire.* London.

———. 1993b. *The Mediterranean World in Late Antiquity.* London.

———. 1997. "Eusebius' *Vita Constantini* and the Construction of Constantine." In Edwards and Swain 1997, 145–74.

Cameron, Averil, and Peter Garnsey. 1998. *The Late Empire, 337–425.* Cambridge Ancient History series, no. 13. Cambridge.

Canivet, P. 1958. *Thérapeutique des maladies Helléniques.* 2 vols. Source Chrétiennes, no. 57. Paris.

———. 1961. "Théodoret et le messalianism." *Revue Mabillon* 51:26–34.

———. 1966. "Le περὶ ἀγάπης de Théodoret de Cyr postface de l'*Histoire Philothée.*" *Studia Patristica* 7:143–58.

———. 1969. "Categories Sociales et Titulaire Laïque et Ecclésiastique dans l'*Histoire Philothée* de Théodoret de Cyr." *Byzantion* 39:209–50.

———. 1977. *Le monachisme Syrien selon Théodoret de Cyr.* Théologie Historique, no. 42. Paris.

Canivet, P., and A. Leroy-Molinghen. 1977–79. *Histoire des moines de Syrie.* Paris.

Chadwick, H. 1951. "Eucharist and Christology in the Nestorian Controversy." *Journal of Theological Studies,* n.s., 2:145–64.

———. 1967. *The Early Church.* Harmondsworth.

———. 1985. "The Ascetic Ideal in the History of the Church." In *Studies in Church History,* ed W. J. Sheils, 1–23. Oxford. Reprinted in *Heresy and Orthodoxy in the Early Church,* Aldershot, 1991.

Chesnut, G. F. 1986. *The First Christian Histories.* Macon, Ga.

Chitty, Derwas. 1966. *The Desert a City.* Oxford.

Clark, E. A. 1999. "Rewriting Early Christian History: Augustine's Representation of Monica." In *Portraits of Spiritual Authority.* ed. J. W. Drijvers and J. W. Watt, 3–23. Leiden.

Clark, Gillian. 2000. "Philosophic Lives and the Philosophic Life: Porphyry and Iamblichus." In Hägg and Rousseau 2000a, 29–51.

Clayton, P. B. 1985. "Theodoret, Bishop of Cyrus, and the Mystery of the

Incarnation in Late Antiochene Theology." Ph.D. diss., Union Theological Seminary, New York. 2 vols.

Coon, L. L. 1997. *Sacred Fictions: Holy Women and Hagiography in Late Antiquity.* Philadelphia.

Cooper, K. 1992. "Insinuations of Womanly Influence: An Aspect of the Christianization of the Roman Aristocracy." *Journal of Roman Studies* 82: 150–64.

Cox, Patricia. 1983. *Biography in Late Antiquity.* Berkeley.

Cunningham, M., and P. Allen, eds. 1998. *Preacher and Audience.* Leiden.

Dagron, G. 1970. "Les moines et la ville: Le monachisme à Constantinople jusqu'au concile de Chalcedoine." *Travaux et Mémoires* 4:229–76.

Dalrymple, W. 1997. *From the Holy Mountain.* London.

Davies, S. L. 1984. "Ascetic Madness." In Smith and Lounibos 1984, 13–26.

Delehaye, Hippolyte. 1923. *Les Saints Stylites.* Studia Hagiographica, no. 14. Brussels.

Devos, P. 1979. "La Structure de l'*Histoire Philothée* de Théodoret de Cyr: Le nombre de chapitres." *Analecta Bollandiana* 97:319–36.

Devreesse, R. 1945. *Le Patriarcat d'Antioche depuis la paix de l'Eglise jusqu'au la conquête arabe.* Paris.

Dodds, E. R. 1965. *Pagan and Christian in an Age of Anxiety.* New York.

Doran, R. 1992. *The Lives of Simeon Stylites.* Translation with introduction. Kalamazoo.

Downey, Glanville. 1961. *A History of Antioch in Syria from Seleucus to the Arab Conquest.* Princeton.

Draguet, R. 1946. "L'inauthenticité du proemium de *l'histoire lausiaque.*" *Le Muséon* 59:529–34.

Drijvers, H. J. W. 1978. "Spätantike Parallelen zur altchristlichen Heiligenverehrung unter besonderer Berücksichtigung des syrischen Stylitenkultus." *Göttinger Orientforschungen* 1:77–113.

———. 1981. "Hellenistic and Oriental Origins." In Hackel 1981, 25–33.

———. 1998. "Syriac Culture in Late Antiquity: Hellenism and Local Traditions." *Mediterraneo Antico* 1.1: 95–113.

Duchesne, L. 1929. *Histoire ancienne de l'Eglise.* 5th ed., vol. 3. Paris.

Dudley, M. 1991. "Danger and Glory: Priesthood in the Writings of John Chrysostom." *Studia Patristica* 27:162–65.

Duff, Tim. 1999. *Plutarch's Lives: Exploring Vice and Virtue.* Oxford.

Dunn, Marilyn. 2000. *The Emergence of Monasticism: from the Desert Fathers to the Early Middle Ages.* Oxford.

Edwards, M. J., and S. Swain, eds. 1997. *Portraits: Biographical Representation in the Greek and Latin Literature of the Roman Empire.* Oxford.

Elliott, A. Goddard. 1987. *Roads to Paradise: Reading the Lives of the Early Saints.* Hanover, N.H.

Elm, S. 1994. *Virgins of God: The Making of Asceticism in Late Antiquity.* Oxford.

Elton, Hugh. Forthcoming. *Cilicia.* Oxford.

Escolan, P. 1999. *Monachisme et Eglise: Le monachisme syrien du IVe au VIIe siècle, un ministère charismatique.* Théologie Historique, no. 109. Paris.

Evans, E. C. 1969. *Physiognomics in the Ancient World.* Transactions of the American Philosophical Society, no. 59, pt. 5. Philadelphia.

Festugière, A. J. 1959. *Antioche paienne et Chrétienne.* Paris.

————. 1960. "Lieux communs littéraires et thèmes de folk-lore dans l'hagiographie primitive." *Wiener Studien* 73:123–52.

————. 1982. *Ephèse et Chalcédoine: Actes des Conciles.* Translated into French. Paris.

Fliche A., and V. Martin, eds. 1948. *Histoire de l'Eglise.* Vol. 4. Paris.

Flusin, Bernard. 1993. "Syméon et les Philologues, ou la mort du Stylite." In *Les saints et leur sanctuaire.* 1–23. Byzantina Sorbonensia, no. 11.

Fouracre, Paul. 1999. "Regulating the Cult of the Saints." In Howard-Johnston and Hayward 1999, 143–65.

Fowden, Garth. 1982. "The Pagan Holy Man in Late Antique Society." *Journal of Hellenic Studies* 102:33–59.

————. 1999. "Religious Communities." In Bowersock, Brown, and Grabar 1999, 82–106.

Francis, J. A. 1995. *Subversive Virtue: Asceticism and Authority in the Second-Century Pagan World.* University Park, Pa.

Frank, Georgia. 1998. "Miracles, Monks, and Monuments: The *Historia Monachorum in Aegypto* as Pilgrims' Tales." In *Pilgrimage and Holy Space in Late Antique Egypt,* ed. David Frankfurter, 483–505. Leiden.

————. 2000. *The Memory of the Eyes: Pilgrims to Living Saints in Christian Late Antiquity.* Berkeley.

Frankfurter, D. 1990. "Stylites and Phallobates: Pillar Religions in Late Antique Syria." *Vigiliae Christianae* 44:168–98.

Fuhrmann, Manfred. 1976. "Die Mönchsgeschichten des Hieronymus: Form-experimente in erzählender Literatur." In *Christianisme et formes littéraires de l'antiquité tardive en Occident,* 41–89. Geneva.

Gahbauer, F. R. 1993. *Die Pentarchietheorie.* Frankfurt.

Gallico, A. 1995. *Teodoreto di Cirro: Storia di Monaci Siri.* Translation into Italian with introduction and notes. Rome.

Garnsey, P. 1996. "Prologomenon to a Study of the Land in the Later Roman Empire." In ENEPΓEIA*: Studies on Ancient History and Epigraphy Presented to H. W. Pleket,* ed. J. H. M. Stubbe, R. A. Tybout, and H. S. Versnel, 135–53. Dutch Monographs on Ancient History and Archaeology, no. 16. Amsterdam.

Goehring, James E. 1992. "The Origins of Monasticism." In *Eusebius, Christianity, and Judaism,* ed. H. W. Attridge and G. Hata, 235–55. Leiden. Reprinted in Goehring 1999, 13–35.

————. 1993. "The Encroaching Desert: Literary Production and Ascetic Space in Early Christian Egypt." *Journal of Early Christian Studies* 1:281–96. Reprinted in Goehring 1999, 73–88.

————. 1999. *Ascetics, Society, and the Desert.* Harrisburg, Pa.

Gould, G. 1993. *The Desert Fathers on Monastic Community.* Oxford.

Gregory, Timothy E. 1979. *Vox Populi.* Columbus.

Gribomont, Jean. 1965. "Le Monachisme au sein de l'Eglise en Syrie et en Cappadoce." *Studia Monastica* 7:7–24.

———. 1981. "Théodoret et les Vies des Pères." *Rivista di Storia e Letteratura Religiosa* 17:45–48.

Griffith, S. 1995. "Asceticism in the Church of Syria: The Hermeneutics of Early Syrian Monasticism." In Wimbush and Valantasis 1995, 220–45.

Grillmeier, A. 1975. *Christ in Christian Tradition.* Trans. J. Bowden. Vol. 1. 2d ed. London.

Grillmeier, A., and H. Bacht. 1953–54. *Das Konzil von Chalkedon.* 3 vols. Würzburg.

Hackel, Sergei, ed. 1981. *The Byzantine Saint.* London.

Hägg, Tomas, and Philip Rousseau, eds. 2000a. *Greek Biography and Panegyric in Late Antiquity.* Berkeley.

———. 2000b. "Introduction: Biography and Panegyric." In Hägg and Rousseau 2000a, 1–28.

Halleux, A. de. 1993. "Le Concile de Chalcedoine." *Revue des Sciences Religieuses* 67:3–18.

Hansen, G. C. 1995. *Sokrates Kirchengeschichte.* Berlin.

Hill, Robert C. 2000. *Theodoret of Cyrus: Commentary on the Psalms 1–72.* Translation with introduction and notes. Washington, D.C.

Hobbes, Thomas. [1651] 1958. *Leviathan.* Introduction by H. W. Schneider. Englewood Cliffs, N.J.

Hofmann, H. 1997. "Von der geistlichen Biographie zur Heiligenlegende: Hagiographie als Historiographie." In *Neues Handbuch der Literaturwissenschaft,* ed. L. J. Engels and H. Hoffman, 403–67. Wiesbaden.

Holl, K. 1908. "Das Fortleben der Volkssprachen in Kleinasien in nachchristlicher Zeit." *Hermes* 43:240–54.

Holum, K. G. 1982. *Theodosian Empresses.* Berkeley.

Honigmann, Ernest. 1947. "The Patriarchate of Antioch: A Revision of Le Quien and the *Notitia Antiochena.*" *Traditio* 5:135–61.

———. 1953. "Theodoret of Cyrrhus and Basil of Seleucia (the Time of Their Death). *Studi E Testi, Patristic Studies* 173:174–84.

Hopwood, K. R. 1994. "The Indigenous Populations of Roman Rough Cilicia." In *X Turk Tarih Kurumu, Kongreye Sunulan Bildiriler,* 337–45. Ankara.

Howard-Johnston, James, and Paul Hayward, eds. 1999. *The Cult of Saints in Late Antiquity and the Early Middle Ages.* Oxford.

Hunt, E. D. 1973. "Palladius of Helenopolis: A Party and Its Supporters in the Church of the Late Fourth Century." *Journal of Theological Studies,* n.s., 24:456–80.

Jackson, Blomfield. [1892]. 1994. *Nicene and Post-Nicene Fathers.* Vol. 3. Ed. P. Schaff and H. Wace. Peabody, Mass.

Jones, A. H. M. 1964. *The Later Roman Empire.* Oxford.

———. 1966. *The Decline of the Ancient World.* London.

———. 1971. *Cities of the Eastern Roman Provinces.* 2d ed. Oxford.

Judge, E. A. 1977. "The Earliest Use of 'Monachos' for Monk and the Origins of Monasticism." *Jahrbuch für Antike und Christentum* 2:72–89.

Kaplan, Michel. 1993. "Le saint, le village, et la cité." *Byzantina Sorbonensia* 11:81–94.

Kazhdan, A. 1995. "Holy and Unholy Miracle Workers." *Byzantine Magic,* ed. H. Maguire, 73–82. Dumbarton Oaks.

Kidd, B. J. 1922. *A History of the Church to* A.D. *461.* Vol. 3. Oxford.

Konstan, D. 1997. *Friendship in the Classical World.* Cambridge.

Konstan, David. 2000. "How to Praise a Friend: St. Gregory of Nazianzus's Funeral Oration for St. Basil the Great." In Hägg and Rousseau 2000a, 160–79.

Krueger, D. 1996. *Symeon the Holy Fool: Leontius' Life and the Late Antique City.* Berkeley.

Krueger, D. 1997a. "Writing as Devotion." *Church History* 66.4: 707–19.

———. 1997b. "Typological Figuration in Theodoret of Cyrrhus." *Journal of Early Christian Studies* 5.3: 393–419.

Lampe, G. W. H., ed. 1961. *A Patristic Greek Lexicon.* Oxford.

Lane Fox, R. 1997. "The *Life of Daniel.*" In Edwards and Swain 1997, 175–225.

Lefkowitz, M. 1981. *Heroines and Hysterics.* London.

———. 1986. *Women in Greek Myth.* London.

Leppin, Hartmut. 1996a. "Zum kirchenpolitischen Kontext von Theodorets Mönchsgeschichte." *Klio* 78:212–30.

———. 1996b. *Von Constantin dem Grossen zu Theodosius II: Das christliche Kaisertum bei den Kirchenhistorikern Socrates, Sozomenus, and Theodoret.* Göttingen.

Liddell, H. G., and R. Scott, eds. 1968. *Greek-English Lexicon.* Revised and augmented by H. S. Jones with the assistance of R. McKenzie. Oxford.

Liebeschuetz, J. H. W. G. 1972. *Antioch: City and Imperial Administration in the Later Roman Empire.* Oxford.

———. 1993. "Ecclesiastical Historians on Their Own Times." *Studia Patristica* 24:151–63.

Lietzmann, Hans. 1908. *Das Leben des Heiligen Symeon Stylites.* Leipzig. German translation of the Syriac *Life of Symeon,* by Heinrich Hilgenfeld. *Texte und Untersuchungen zur Geschichte der altchristlichen Literatur* Series 3, vol. 2, part 4.

Lim, R. 1991. "Theodoret of Cyrus and the Speakers in the Greek Dialogues." *Journal of Hellenic Studies* 111:181–82.

———. 1995. *Public Disputation, Power, and Social Order in Late Antiquity.* Berkeley.

Livingstone, E. A. 1997. *The Oxford Dictionary of the Christian Church.* 3d ed. Oxford.

McCollough, C. T. 1985. "Theodoret of Cyrus as Biblical Interpreter and the Presence of Judaism in the Later Roman Empire." *Studia Patristica* 13: 327–34.

MacDermot, V. 1971. *The Cult of the Seer in the Ancient Middle East.* Berkeley.

McGroarty, K., ed. 2001. *Eklogai: Studies in Honour of Thomas Finan and Gerard Watson.* Maynooth, Ireland.

McLynn, N. 1998. "A Self-Made Holy Man: The Case of Gregory Nazianzen." *Journal of Early Christian Studies* 6.3: 463–83.

MacMullen, R. 1966. "Provincial Languages in the Roman Empire." *American Journal of Philology* 87:1–17.

Mansfield, J. and Runia, D. T. 1997. *Aëtiana: The Method and Intellectual Context of a Doxographer.* Vol. 1. Leiden.

Markus, R. 1990. *The End of Ancient Christianity.* Cambridge.

Martin, Annick. 1993. "Figures du 'je' et jeux de figures dans les *Apologies* d'Athanase: Aux Antipodes de l'autobiographie." In *L'Invention de l'autobiographie d'Hésiode à Saint Augustin,* ed. M.-F. Baslez, P. Hoffmann, and L. Pernot, 147–54. Etudes de Littérature Ancienne, no. 5.

Mayer, W. 1998. "John Chrysostom: Extraordinary Preacher, Ordinary Audience." In Cunningham and Allen 1998, 105–37.

Meredith, A. 1998. "The Three Cappadocians on Beneficence." In Cunningham and Allen 1998, 89–104.

Millar, Fergus. 1971. "Paul of Samosata, Zenobia, and Aurelian: The Church, Local Culture, and Political Allegiance in Third-Century Syria." *Journal of Roman Studies* 61:1–17.

———. 1993. *The Roman Near East, 31 B.C.–A.D. 337.* Cambridge, Mass.

———. 1998a. "Il ruole delle lingue semitiche nel vicino oriente tardo-romano (V–VI secolo)." *Mediterraneo Antico* 1:71–93.

———. 1998b. "Ethnic Identity in the Roman Near East, 325–450: Language, Religion, and Culture." *Mediterranean Archaeology* 11:159–76.

Miller, Patricia Cox. 2000. "Strategies of Representation in Collective Biography." In Hägg and Rousseau 2000a, 209–54.

Mitchell, S. 1993. *Anatolia: Land, Men, and Gods in Asia Minor.* Vol. 2: *The Rise of the Church.* Oxford.

Mitchell, S., and G. Greatrex, eds. 2000. *Ethnicity and Culture in Late Antiquity.* Cardiff.

Moine, Nicole. 1980. "Melaniana." *Recherches Augustiniennes* 15:3–79.

Momigliano, A. [1971] 1993. *The Development of Greek Biography.* Expanded ed. Cambridge, Mass.

———. 1987. "Ancient Biography and the Study of Religion in the Roman Empire." In *On Pagans, Jews, and Christians,* ed. A. Momigliano, 159–77. Middletown, Conn.

———. 1990. *The Classical Foundations of Modern Historiography.* Berkeley.

Munitiz, Joseph. 1981. "Self-Canonisation: The 'Partial Account' of Nikephoros Blemmydes." In Hackel 1981, 164–68.

Murphy, F. X. 1947. "Melania the Elder: A Biographical Note." *Traditio* 5: 59–77.

Murray, R. 1975. *Symbols of Church and Kingdom: A Study in Early Syriac Tradition.* Cambridge.

Naaman, R. Paul. 1971. *Théodoret de Cyr et le monastère de Saint Maroun.* Beirut.

Nau, F. 1909. "La naissance de Nestorius." *Revue de l'Orient chétien* 4:424–26.

Newman, John Henry. [1873] 1970. *Historical Sketches.* 3 vols. Westminster, Md. See 2:307–62 on Theodoret.

Nock, A. D. 1933. *Conversion: The Old and the New in Religion from Alexander the Great to Augustine of Hippo.* Oxford.

Norris, Frederick W. 2000. "Your Honor, My Reputation: St. Gregory of Nazianzus' Funeral Oration on St. Basil the Great." In Hägg and Rousseau 2000a, 140–59.

O'Keeffe, J. J. 2000. "'A Letter That Killeth': Towards a Reassessment of Antiochene Exegesis, or Diodore, Theodore, and Theodoret on the Psalms." *Journal of Early Christian Studies* 8.1: 83–104.

O'Neill, J. C. 1989. "The Origins of Monasticism." In *The Making of Orthodoxy,* ed. Rowan Williams, 270–87. Cambridge.

Parmentier, L. 1998. *Theodoret Kirchengeschichte.* 3d ed. Ed. G. C. Hansen. Berlin.

Patlagean, E. 1983. "Ancient Byzantine Hagiography and Social History." In Wilson 1983, 101–21.

Paton, W. R. 1916–18. *The Greek Anthology.* Cambridge, Mass.

Peeters, P. 1920. "La legende de saint Jacques de Nisibe." *Analecta Bollandiana* 38:285–373.

———. 1942. "S. Symeon Stylites et ses premiers biographes." *Analecta Bollandiana* 61:29–71.

———. 1950. *Le tréfonds oriental de l'hagiographie byzantine.* Brussels.

Price, Richard M. 1985a. *A History of the Monks of Syria by Theodoret of Cyrrhus.* Kalamazoo.

———. 1985b. "Holy Men's Letters of Rebuke." *Studia Patristica* 16:50–53.

Quasten, J. 1960. *Patrologie.* Vol. 3. Utrecht.

Rapp, C. 1998. "Comparison, Paradigm, and the Case of Moses in Panegyric and Hagiography." In *Propaganda of Power,* ed. M. Whitby, 277–98. Leiden.

———. 1999. "'For Next to God You Are My Salvation': Reflections on the Rise of the Holy Man in Late Antiquity." In Howard-Johnston and Hayward 1999. 63–81.

Richard, M. 1935. "L'Activité littéraire de Théodoret avant le Concile d'Ephèse." *Revue des Sciences Philosophiques et Théologiques* 24:83–106.

———. 1946. "Théodoret, Jean d'Antioche, et les moines d'Orient." *Mélanges de Science Réligieuse* 3:147–56.

Rousseau, P. 1971. "The Spiritual Authority of the 'Monk-Bishop'. Eastern Elements in Some Western Hagiography of the Fourth and Fifth Centuries." *Journal of Theological Studies,* n.s., 22:380–419.

Rousseau, Philip. 1978. *Ascetics, Authority, and the Church in the Age of Jerome and Cassian.* Oxford.

———. 1997. "Eccentrics and Coenobites in the Late Roman East." *Byzantinische Forschungen* 24:35–50.

———. 1998. "The Identity of the Ascetic Master in the *Historia Religiosa* of Theodoret of Cyrrhus: A New *Paideia?*" *Mediterranean Archaeology* 11: 229–44.

———. 2000. "Antony as Teacher in the Greek *Life.*" In Hägg and Rousseau 2000a, 89–109.

Rubenson, S. 2000. "Philosophy and Simplicity: The Problem of Classical Education in Early Christian Biography. In Hägg and Rousseau 2000a, 110–39.

Russell, D. 1998. "The Panegyrists and Their Teachers." In Whitby 1998, 17–49.

Russell, D., and N. G. Wilson. 1981. *Menander Rhetor.* Oxford.

Ste. Croix, G. E. M. de. 1981. *Class Struggle in the Ancient Greek World.* London.

Sartre, M. 1991. *L'Orient Romain.* Paris.

Schwartz, E. 1922–23. *Concilium Universale Chalcedonense.* Vol. 1, part 4. Berlin.

———. 1936. *Concilium Universale Chalcedonense.* Vol. 5, part 2. Berlin.

Smith, R. C., and J. Lounibos, eds. 1984. *Pagan and Christian Anxiety: A Response to E. R. Dodds.* Lanham, Md.

Sobré, J. M. 1987. "The Voice of God in Medieval Catalan Literature." *Semiotica* 63:143–49.

Spadavecchia, C. 1985. "The Rhetorical Tradition in the Letters of Theodoret of Cyrus." In *From Late Antiquity to Early Byzantium: Proceedings of the Byzantinological Symposium in the Sixteenth International Eirene Conference,* ed. Vladimir Vavrinek, 249–52. Prague.

Steininger, C. 1997. *Die ideale christliche Frau.* Munich.

Stewart, Columba. 1991. *"Working the Earth of the Heart": The Messalian Controversy in History, Texts, and Language to* A.D. *431.* Oxford.

Swain, S. 1997. "Biography and Biographic in the Literature of the Roman Empire." In Edwards and Swain 1997, 1–37.

Tate, Georges. 1992. *Les Campagnes de la Syrie du Nord du IIe au VIIe siècle.* Vol. 1. Paris.

Tchalenko, Georges. 1953. *Villages antiques de la Syrie du Nord: Le Massif du Bélus à l'époque romaine.* 3 vols. Paris.

Tompkins, I. G. 1995. "Problems of Dating and Pertinence in Some Letters of Theodoret of Cyrrhus." *Byzantion* 65:176–95.

Trombley, F. R. 1995. *Hellenic Religion and Christianization c. 370–529.* Vol. 2, 2d ed. Leiden.

Turner, C. H. 1905. "The *Lausiac History* of Palladius." *Journal of Theological Studies* 6:321–55.

Urbainczyk, T. 1997a. *Socrates of Constantinople.* Ann Arbor.

———. 1997b. "Observations on the Differences between the Church Histories of Socrates and Sozomen." *Historia* 46.3: 355–73.

———. 2000. "The Devil Spoke Syriac to Me: Theodoret in Syria." In Mitchell and Greatrex 2000, 253–65.

———. 2001. "Cloth and Sackcloth: Theodoret and the *Religious History.*" *Studia Patristica* 35:167–71.

Van Dam, R. 1993. *Saints and their Miracles in Late Antique Gaul.* Princeton.

Van Uytfange, M. 1981. "La controverse biblique et patristique autour du miracle, et ses repercussions sur l'hagiographie dans l'Antiquité tardive et le haut Moyen Age Latin." In *Hagiographie: Cultures et Société IVe–XIIe siècles: Actes du Colloque organizé à Nanterre et à Paris, 2–5 Mai 1979,* ed. E. Patlagean and P. Riché, 205–33. Paris.

———. 1993. "L'Hagiographie: Un 'genre' chrétien ou antique tardif?" *Analecta Bollandiana* 111:135–88.

Viller, M., Cavallera, F., and de Guibert, J. 1980. *Dictionnaire de Spiritualité.* Vol. 10. Paris.

Vööbus, Arthur. 1960. *History of Asceticism in the Syrian Orient.* Vol. 2. Corpus Scriptorum Christianorum Orientalium, no. 197, subsidiary vol. 17. Louvain.

Walbank, F. W. 1967. *A Historical Commentary on Polybius.* Vol. 2. Oxford.

Wallace-Hadrill, D. S. 1982. *Christian Antioch.* Cambridge.

Wardman, A. E. 1971. "Plutarch's Method in the *Lives.*" *Classical Quarterly,* n.s., 21:254–61.

Whitby, Mary, ed. 1998. *The Propaganda of Power: The Role of Panegyric in Late Antiquity.* Leiden.

White, Carolinne. 1998. *Early Christian Lives.* Translated with introduction and notes. Harmondsworth.

Wickham, L. 1993. "Teachings about God and Christ in the *Liber Graduum.*" In *Logos: Festschrift für Luise Abramowski,* 486–98. Berlin.

Wilson, Stephen, ed. 1983. Introduction to *Saints and Their Cults,* 1–53. Cambridge.

Wimbush, V. L. 1986. "Renunciation towards Social Engineering: An Apologia for the Study of Asceticism in Greco-Roman Antiquity." In *Occasional Papers of the Institute for Antiquity and Christianity,* no. 8, 3–20. Claremont.

Wimbush, V. L., and R. Valantasis, eds. 1995. *Asceticism.* Oxford.

Woodman, A. J. 1988. *Rhetoric in Classical Historiography.* Beckenham.

Woods, D. 2001. "Some *Eunapiana.*" In McGroarty 2001, 85–132.

Young, F. 1983. *From Nicaea to Chalcedon.* London.

———. 1991. *The Making of the Creeds.* London.

———. 1997. *Biblical Exegesis and the Formation of Christian Culture.* Cambridge.

Index

Abraham (subject of *RH* 17), 33, 71, 74, 77, 81, 118, 122–25
Abraham (companion of Palladius), 82
Acacius (bishop of Beroea), 25, 121, 124
Acepsimas (subject of *RH* 15), 82, 96, 120, 121, 144
Agapetus of Apamea, 121, 122, 124
Alexander (bishop of Antioch), 128
Alexander (bishop of Hierapolis), 25, 26
Alexandria, 54, 147, 149, 150, 151; Cyril, bishop of, 12; Dioscorus, bishop of, 22; disputes with Antioch, 4, 10, 32; major see, 15; role in the Councils of Ephesus and Chalcedon, 23–28; Theophilus, bishop of, 12
Ambrose (bishop of Milan), 31
Ammianus (friend of holy man Eusebius), 48, 84, 119, 129
Antioch, 54, 73, 106, 115, 119, 124, 129, 131, 137, 139, 147, 150; Cyrrhus and, 21–23; John Chrysostom and, 12, 15; language of, 15, 16; in religious disputes, 4, 5, 10, 23–28, 32, 37; Theodoret in, 14–21; in works of Theodoret, 31, 35–39, 46
Antiochus (ascetic), 81
Antoninus (ascetic), 81
Antony, 43, 44, 45, 69, 83, 124, 144. See also *Life of Antony*

Antony (author of Greek life of Symeon Stylites), 100, 101, 106
Apamea, 21, 121
Aphrahat (subject of *RH* 8), 70, 77, 93, 104, 131, 132, 138, 141, 144
Aphthonius, 72, 121
Arcadius (emperor), 11, 12
Arianism, 36. *See also* Arians; Heresy
Arians, 30, 81, 124. *See also* Arianism; Heresy
Asceticism, 7, 13, 14; extremes of, 135; forms of, 35, 39, 47–51, 75, 76, 80–88; results of, 56, 89–94, 145; Syrian, 6, 95–102, 150; weeping as part of, 110. *See also* Ascetics; Holy men and women; Monks
Ascetics: relations with Church, 8, 35, 115–29; relations with Theodoret and his family, 20, 130–42; in Syria 14; use of term, 13. *See also* Holy men and women; Monks
Asclepius (subject of *RH* 22), 81, 86
Ashbrook Harvey, S., 99, 101
Astrion, 104
Athanasius, 43, 44
Augustine, 103, 138

Baradatos (subject of *RH* 27), 25, 26, 60, 82, 89, 102, 129
Barbarians, 11, 13, 78, 96, 99, 111; have some knowledge, 16; Persians are, 77
Basil (disciple of Marcianus), 83

165

ons regulating, 27; other lives of,
40–51; *Religious History* about, 32–
39; 67–79
Monophysites, 28
Moses (ascetic), 81
Moses (of the Old Testament), 61,
122

Nestorianism. *See* Nestorius
Nestorius, 13, 23–28, 151
Newman, J. H., 92
Nicerte (Theodoret's monastery), 21
Nicomedia, 25
Nomus, 19

Olympius (rude Roman), 118
Omeros (village), 82
On Divine Love, 52, 59–64, 67, 105,
129, 144
Orestes (governor of Alexandria),
149
Ovodianus, 104
Oxyrhynchus, 48, 108

Pagans, 30, 38, 41–42, 99
Palestine, 43, 59, 87, 88, 126
Palladius (ascetic), 82, 96
Palladius (author of *Lausiac History*),
39, 43, 50, 57, 108
Panegyric, 57, 58, 90. *See also* Eulogy
Paul (apostle), 55, 62, 77, 101, 144
Paul of Thebes, 69. See also *Life of
Paul of Thebes*
Peeters, P., 21
Pergamius, 104
Periodeutes, 117n
Persia, Magi of, 30
Persians, 77, 96, 151
Peter (apostle), 62, 101, 129
Peter the Galatian (subject of *RH* 9),
18, 82, 93, 104–5, 131–34, 138–39,
141
Photius, 16, 19
Plotinus. See *Life of Plotinus*
Plutarch, 41, 46, 57

Polychronius (subject of *RH* 24–25),
86, 117
Pontus, 59, 70, 87
Porphyry, 41–42
Price, Richard, 34, 60, 90–91
Priests, 9, 116, 118, 120. *See also*
Bishops; Clergy; Clerics
Proclus (bishop of Constantinople),
26
Prologue, 51, 52–59, 63, 67
Publius (subject of *RH* 5), 70, 72,
84–87
Pulcheria, 12, 24, 27

Reader, 20, 140. *See also* Clergy;
Clerics
Religious History (*RH*): importance
of, 3; information on holy men in,
4; information on Theodoret in, 7–
8; language of, 5; reply to Egyptian
works, 5; survey of, 32–39; terms
used in, 13; title of, 33–34
Romanos (subject of *RH* 11), 82 105
Romans, 16, 96, 118
Rome, 11, 15, 38, 124, 150
Rousseau, P., 81, 85, 124, 127
Rufinus, history of, 43

Sabinus (companion of Marcianus),
83, 86, 106
Salamanes (subject of *RH* 19), 34, 82,
96, 121, 144
Socrates (the church historian), 4, 30,
31, 43–44, 149
Socrates (the philosopher), 55
Song of Songs, 61, 62
Sozomen (the church historian), 4,
30, 31, 39, 43–44
Stylitism, 14, 95–102, 147. *See also*
Symeon Stylites
Sulpicius Severus, 42, 54, 124, 152.
See also *Life of Martin of Tours;*
Martin of Tours
Symeon Stylites (subject of *RH* 26),
7, 8, 14, 25–26, 38, 44, 60, 70, 72,

Index Locorum

Symeon Stylites (*continued*)
26.16–17: 99
26.21: 105, 107, 133
26.25: 72
26.27: 38

Baradatus
27: 25, 60, 91, 93n, 107
27.1: 35n, 56n, 57, 89
27.2: 91n
27.3: 82, 129

Thalelaeus
28: 91, 93n, 107, 125, 131
28.4: 71, 76n
28.5: 82

Marana and Cyra
29: 93n, 103n, 108, 125, 131
29.1: 107, 111
29.2: 71, 87, 108

29.5: 109, 125
29.7: 108

Domnina
30: 93n, 103n, 108, 125, 131
30.1: 109
30.2: 110
30.3: 71, 81, 109, 117, 128
30.5: 87
30.5–6: 59
30.6: 88

On Divine Love: 52, 59–64, 105
ODL.1: 61
ODL.3: 111
ODL.5: 61, 62
ODL.10: 129n
ODL.15: 33
ODL.17: 62
ODL.19: 61, 62
ODL.21: 63